2004 POETK

ONCE UPON A RHYME

IMAGINATION FOR
A NEW GENERATION

Bridgend

Edited by Allison Dowse

Young Writers

First published in Great Britain in 2004 by:
Young Writers
Remus House
Coltsfoot Drive
Peterborough
PE2 9JX
Telephone: 01733 890066
Website: www.youngwriters.co.uk

SB ISBN 1 84460 444 6

Foreword

Young Writers was established in 1991 and has been passionately devoted to the promotion of reading and writing in children and young adults ever since. The quest continues today. Young Writers remains as committed to engendering the fostering of burgeoning poetic and literary talent as ever.

This year's Young Writers competition has proven as vibrant and dynamic as ever and we are delighted to present a showcase of the best poetry from across the UK. Each poem has been carefully selected from a wealth of *Once Upon A Rhyme* entries before ultimately being published in this, our twelfth primary school poetry series.

Once again, we have been supremely impressed by the overall high quality of the entries we have received. The imagination, energy and creativity which has gone into each young writer's entry made choosing the best poems a challenging and often difficult but ultimately hugely rewarding task - the general high standard of the work submitted amply vindicating this opportunity to bring their poetry to a larger appreciative audience.

We sincerely hope you are pleased with our final selection and that you will enjoy *Once Upon A Rhyme Bridgend* for many years to come.

Contents

Oldcastle Junior School

Ellie Rice (7)	17
Ieuan Loughran (11)	18
Bethan Sian Hocking (10)	19
William Thomas (11)	20
Catherine Felton (11)	21
Hayley Norris (11)	22
Ceri-Anne Thomas (9)	23
Bethan Jehu (9)	24
Byoung-In Min (8)	24
Daniel Catton (9)	25
Rachael Sparrow (7)	25
Josh Harris (9)	26
Morgan Neagle (7)	26
Amy Roberts (9)	27
Charlotte Barrett (8)	27
Nathan Jones (10)	28
Adam Davies (8)	28
Elinor Thomas (8)	29
Charles Cottrell (9)	29
Hollie Morgan (9)	30
Tomas Morgan (9)	31
Martha Parrish (10)	32
Huw Lewis (9)	33
Reuben Fisher (10)	34
Lewis Down (9)	35
Kate Jones (8)	36
Jessie Rebecca Hathaway (9)	37
Kate Manning (10)	38
Amy Sandford (8)	38
Conor Lynn (9)	39
Adam Brown (7)	39
Nia Williams (10)	40
Bethan Mason (8)	40
Ryan Stacey (10)	41
Lois John (10)	41
Ellie Jane Morgan (8)	42
Alys Clark (8)	42

Pencoed Junior School

Ian Richards (9)	43
Susan James (10)	43
Ieuan Parrish (9)	43
Ricky Elward (9)	44
Leum Williams (9)	44
Sophie Thompson (9)	45
Luke Phillips (11)	45
Phillipa Lauren Smith (11)	46
Hannah James (11)	46
Cerys Hoskins (11)	47
Whitney Brown (10)	47
Rhian Simmonds (10)	48
Scott Henwood (9)	48
Jobe Aaron Parrish (10)	49
Samantha Johns (11)	49
Samantha McLaren-Brown (9)	50
Louise Howard (9)	50
Lauren Cox (10)	51
Alex Rice (9)	51
Holly McHugh (10)	52
Dominic Luff (10)	52
Jessica Brown (9)	53
Jack Hiscocks (10)	53
Cerys Thomas (10)	54
Hayley Selway (10)	54
Rebecca Baker (11)	55
Ross Hall (10)	55
Joseph Housley (11)	56
Elinôr Clark (10)	56
Leah Andrews (10)	57
Christian Alex Williams (10)	58
Ieuan Griffiths (9)	58
Bleddyn Jury (10)	59
Kelly Tucker (11)	59
Autumn Bevan (11)	60
Naomi Jenkins (10)	60
Salimah Jackson (10)	61
Shauna Blake (11)	61
Nikki Letitia Morgan (10)	62
Hannah-Marie Jenkins (10)	62

Carly Hale (11)	63
Thomas James Shakespeare (10)	63
Natasha John (11)	64
Ria Hearne (10)	64
Matthew Alan Coleman (11)	65
Rebecca Jayne Stuckey (10)	65
Dylan White (10)	66
Amy Taylor (11)	66
Victoria Raymond (10)	67
Bethan Williams (11)	68
Stephen Jones (10)	68
Liam Callaghan (11)	69
Rhiannon Pritchard (11)	69
Christopher Hind (11)	70
Michael Cotter-Jones (10)	70
Jodie Maria Parsons (11)	71
Abigail Emily Fitches (10)	72

Pen-Y-Fai CW Primary School

Annie Slennett (8)	73
Emma Oakley (7)	73
Charlotte Price (7)	73
Eleri Thomas (7)	74
Dominic Roberts (8)	74
Nia David (8)	74
Rhys Pascoe (7)	75
Ellie Gilhooley (7)	75
Victoria Leyshon (8)	75
Rhiannon Edwards (10)	76
Alexandra Leyshon (9)	76
Francesca Upton (10)	77
Myriam Hassan (10)	77
Elinor Thomas (10)	77
Alexander Franklin (9)	78
Laura-Jayne Martin (10)	78
Catrin Stephenson (9)	79
Jordon Coombes (10)	79
Hayley Thomas (9)	80
Claire Rowe (9)	80
Samuel McColgan (10)	81
Ryan Williams (9)	81

Luc Thomas (10)	82
Lewis Jon Campbell (8)	82
Luke Williams (9)	82
Morgan Parry (8)	83
Cameron Breheny (8)	83
Lauren Sheppard (8)	83
Nia Elizabeth Gregory (7)	84
Rhiannon McColgan (7)	84
Holly Picton (8)	84
Marco Jones (7)	85
Nia Parry (8)	85
Katie Bellis (8)	85
Emma Sue Davies (8)	86
George Morgan (8)	86
Sebastian Waters-Hussain (8)	86
Lauren Bigley (8)	87
Alys Davies (8)	87
Jack McEachen (7)	87
Kathryn Hof (9)	88
Rosie Upton (8)	88
Jac David (9)	89
Samantha Keagle (9)	89
Jonathan Westrop (9)	90
Alexander Kemble (8)	90
Ellen Devereux (9)	91
Ben Green (10)	91
Mark Byron Ennis (10)	92
Jack Davies (11)	93
Yacoob Rossaye (11)	94
Holly Hopkins (9)	94
Abigail Trigg (10)	95
Scott Downie (10)	95
Scott Walton (10)	96
Adam Leppard (10)	96
Adam Lee Griffin (11)	97
Bethan Pascoe (11)	97
Eleri Pritchard (10)	98
Morgan Owen (11)	98
Jasmine Gill (10)	99
Kelly Oakley (11)	99

St John's School, Porthcawl

Emily Whittle (9)	100
Dylan Hopkins (8)	100
Tom Brown (8)	101
Ross Murray (8)	101
Henry Thomas Smout (9)	102
Alice Williams (11)	102
Samantha Richardson (9)	103
Michael Raymond (9)	103
Joe Strong (9)	104
Callum Hawker (8)	104
Verity Smout (11)	105
Elliot Jones (8)	105
Daniel Shearer (9)	106
Francesca Groom (9)	106
Isaac Lake (11)	107
Elan Edry (8)	107
George Mead (9)	108
Callum Williamson (10)	108
Ieuan Briers (10)	109
Theo Clarke (9)	109
Aaron James (9)	110
Joe Clarke (10)	111
Dylan Griffiths (10)	112
Bradley John (11)	112
James Kearle (9)	113

St Mary's Catholic Primary School, Bridgend

Joshua Faitas (8)	113
Roisín Ellis (8)	114
William Austin (8)	114
Bethany Louise Hammond (7)	114
Jordan Ryan (8)	115
Catherine Gardiner (9)	115
Evan Lister (8)	115
Zoe-Marie Harrison (9)	116
James Stephens (7)	116
Gervaise Turbervill (10)	117
Emily Read (8)	117
Jessica Williams (8)	118
Laurie Williams (8)	118

West Park Primary School

The Poems

Toothbrush

I sit in a glass every night
When morning comes
I have a fright
I see a big black cave
With lots of white rocks
I feel I'm a slave
I'm slowly losing my pride
There's a pink snake that gets in my way
This makes it even harder every day
My job is to clean
I think this is so mean
They drown me with water
I wish this time would get shorter
Morning is over
But then comes the night
It all happens again
Oh what a fright!

Thomas Watkins (10)
Heol-y-Cyw Primary School

Trees

The wind takes my leaves,
The coldness makes me sneeze,
The ice and snow make me freeze,
But I am still a tree.

When the seasons change,
My leaves change colour,
Red, orange, yellow and brown,
The children play without a frown.

Rebecca Pope (10)
Heol-y-Cyw Primary School

Me A Tree

Me a tree
please don't cut me
if you try I'll call
the bumblebees

Me a tree
every autumn my hair falls down
all sorts of colours
even brown

Me a tree
I am big and tall
and my friend is
short and small

Me a tree
I hear a sound
as I look around
I'm all alone.

Johnathan Cooper (10)
Heol-y-Cyw Primary School

Neil Jenkins

Target hitter
Ball smacker
Brilliant kicker.

Money maker
Tri-scorer
Number 10
Rugby jersey.

Guess who?

He's the best.

Daniel Lee Yaw (11)
Heol-y-Cyw Primary School

Fire Mountain

A land burner
A metal warmer
A fire maker
A man killer
A rock blaster
A house melter
A home destroyer
An egg fryer
A hot warmer
A high mountain
Hot lava.

Owen Davies (10)
Heol-y-Cyw Primary School

Who Am I?

A huge crier,
    A food hater,
        A milk lover,
A bed dreamer,
    A blanket chewer,
        A dummy sucker,
A nappy screamer,
    A toy player,
        A people hugger,
I travel in a pram,
    I'm a . . .

Answer: a baby.

Rhiannon Ames (11)
Heol-y-Cyw Primary School

Ouch!

I don't like being a carpet,
I am full of bruises and cuts,
I am dull, I am the same colour all the time, *blue!*
Smelly, like a dirty mutt.

Why can't I be a wall?
All the games on my face,
Then I live in the hall,
All I need is some space.

All of the boys jump on me,
The tables kick and hit,
Why can't they leave me be?
They hurt when they sit.

Mrs Neil hurts with her heels,
The children and teachers are very nice,
I am glad the chairs are not made from steel,
I wish I could eat rice.

All the mud goes on me by their feet,
I wish I was white as a sheet,
When the light goes off I know it is night,
Then it is a great big fright.

Now there's light,
I am glad,
I am glad it is not night,
The children go mad!

Kelly Underhill (10)
Heol-y-Cyw Primary School

Hairy Giraffe

There once was a hairy giraffe
Who went down the street for a laugh
He caught a bad cold
But he wasn't bold
So he went home and jumped in the bath.

Danielle Perry (10)
Heol-y-Cyw Primary School

Who Am I?

A forest walker
An evening crier
An animal stalker
A grey beast
A sharp-fanged monster
A good smeller
A long fluffy tailer
A harvest moon watcher
A hunter escaper
    I am a wolf
        Hear my call.

Katie Gore (9)
Heol-y-Cyw Primary School

The Stallion

The stallion of the group was a bay
And his mare a grey.

They will gallop around day after day
In the long green grass in the meadow.

The foals will jump, jump and play
Yes, the foals will jump, jump and play
All day, all day.

Then when we have tea
They will play on the sand
And in the sea.

Then when the sun goes down,
And the moon comes up
They will come back to the valley
And wait until the new day.

Elizabeth Lewis (10)
Llangan Primary School

Brother And Sister

I think my brother's really mean
His brain is the size of a kidney bean.

I think my sister's a little bit calm
But most of all she uses lip balm.

Best of all I love to fight
Even though they squeeze me tight.

They sometimes hit me really hard
I love to smack them with a card.

Now we're all sitting quietly
We love to squeeze each other tightly.

Even though they hit me together
I'll always love them forever and ever.

Melissa Lewis (9)
Llangan Primary School

Who

Who makes his mum get up in the morning?
You've got it - me.
Who makes his son wash his lorry?
You've got it - my father.
Who makes me look after her son?
You've got it - my sister.
Who makes me put away all my nephew's toys?
You've got it - my mum.
Who makes me play with him all the time?
You've got it - my nephew.

Mathew Newman (7)
Llangan Primary School

Ten Things Found In A Viking's Pocket

A chipped bit of shiny
stone
A smooth bit of animal
bone

A snail shell from the
sea
A sharp stinger from a
honeybee

A pencil wrapped in green
weed
A big bag of sunflower
seed

A coin shining in the
light
A little snowflake glinting
bright.

Scarlett Barton (8)
Llangan Primary School

There's A Horse In My Bedroom

There's a horse in my bedroom,
His ears as thick as rope,
I wake up in the night,
And he starts to throw the soap,
When I go to ride him he starts to write a note,
But when I get back he's riding in a boat.

Laura Howells (9)
Llangan Primary School

Look Out, Look Out

Look out, look out
There's a sprout about.
Look out, look out
Into the dark night.
Look out, look out
There's a train that goes
Clickety-clack, clickety-clack.
Look out, look out
There's a dangerous dad about.

Ieuan Morgan (7)
Llangan Primary School

Spooky Spectacular

One dark night
A bright spooky spectacular
Sets off for flight.
In the shadows
Up higher
You will see
A distant flyer.

Charlie Foster (8)
Llangan Primary School

Free

Wild horses could never be tamed
They live like the wind
They live like the rain
How much I love them
I know they should be free
Free like the wind
And the rolling sea.

Lauren Gulwell (10)
Llangan Primary School

She

Who loves me? She
Who will help me? She
Who will be my best friend? She
Who is kind? She
Who will be like me? She

Who will hurt me? Not she
Who will kick me? Not she
Who will hate me? Not she
Who will not like me? Not she
Who will be horrible? Not she

Who is she?
My mum is she.

Katie Bugler (9)
Llangan Primary School

My Dad

My dad is a farmer
He works all day
Feeding the animals
With corn and hay.

He drives a tractor
And a Land Rover too
I think it will break down some day
Do you?

The sheep are fat
And in the pen
We are lambing soon
I'm not sure when.

Elliott Rees (8)
Llangan Primary School

Christmas Time

Snowy Christmas is here,
And in Wales it sometimes doesn't occur,
Sitting around the fire,
Saying my sister's a huge liar,
Sitting at the table watching turkey being cut,
Instead of going to Pizza Hut,
Opening my stocking on my bed,
Thinking about what my mum just said,
Watching a beautiful shooting star,
And daydreaming about me in a blue convertible car,
For Santa I'm leaving mince pies and milk,
He will come when I'm under my quilt,

At the end of the day
I look up to God and pray,
'Thank you for making Christmas come,
My family and I had so much fun.'

Charlotte Morgan (9)
Llangan Primary School

Why?

'Why is the sky blue?' I asked
'Why is the grass green?' I asked
'Why are the clouds white?' I asked
'Why are the stars gold?' I asked
'Who made the sky?' I asked
'Who made the grass?' I asked
'Who made the clouds?' I asked
'Who made the stars?' I asked
'God made all,'
He replied.

Hannah Diment (10)
Llangan Primary School

The Family

I think my brother is the worst of the lot,
Most of all he loses the plot.

My sister is the cheekiest of them all,
I hope she trips and has a massive fall.

Our father is the smelliest out of all of us,
I doubt they'll let him on the bus.

Our mother is very bossy,
But she can still be very flossy.

The dog runs around with his tail under his bum,
But sometimes he can be lots of fun.

Well, I'm just a perfect little girl,
And I haven't even got one little curl.

Elizabeth Luke (10)
Llangan Primary School

Mountains and Volcanoes

Mountains and volcanoes
go to war in the night
and give each other a terrible fright
they've got no hands and arms
at the top they've got little holes.

They explode and throw
out lava and rocks
covering everything in the way
when they miss each other
they spoil other things.

Scott Laken (8)
Llangan Primary School

Cats

Wherever you go
They are always around
Tiptoeing behind you
Not making a sound

Wherever you go
They are always there
Sussing you out
Giving you a long hard stare

They watch every move you're making
They're always ready to pounce
All they really do
Is hang around the house.

Alayna Davies (10)
Llangan Primary School

Life On A Farm

I'm a girl who lives on a farm
I don't think that should do any harm

I wake up in the morning to feed the sheep
I give them some food, quite a heap

I feed the cows after school
I think it's fun and rather cool

I have some chickens, a dog too
They wake you up with a 'cock a doodle do'

I have no horses or any pigs
They're rather dirty and give you a kick.

Megan Thomas (10)
Llangan Primary School

A Spell Of Trouble

I can do anything with a spell of trouble,
Even turn people into frogs,
Helpless little frogs,
Or maybe rats and cats
And dogs and hogs.
I can make my own cauldron,
Then do evil spells.
I can do anything with a spell of trouble,
Yes, anything!
I can make a castle,
A dark, evil castle,
All for me!
Yes, I can do anything with a spell of trouble.

Rebecca Lewis (9)
Llangan Primary School

Family

I have two sisters, old and young
One of them's naughty and the other's fun.

I have one dad
I have one mum
They are great parents
They are great fun!

All of the time I think about family,
Whether or not I'm sad or happy.

They are a great family
I'm really, really happy!

Rachel Griffiths (10)
Llangan Primary School

Nature

Nature, nature all around
Nature, nature on the ground

Nature, nature come to me
Nature, nature in the sea

Nature, nature big and small
Nature, nature on the wall

Nature, nature all the world
Nature, nature straight and curled

How did God really make nature?

Daniel Lewis (9)
Llangan Primary School

Sunrise, Sunset On The Field

As I walk on the field,
All its glory is revealed.
As the sun begins to rise,
I feel a sudden surprise.
I walk and walk . . .
I go on for miles,
As I go the time rolls by,
I think I'm going to cry.
As the sun begins to set,
I think of how we met.

Christopher Tune (10)
Llangan Primary School

Bird Of Prey

Bird of prey hovering round,
Looking straight down to the ground,
Sees some mice then looks twice,
And dives from the sky.
His beady eyes staring hard,
The mother mouse is trying to guard
The little baby mice.
The bird of prey is on his way,
Whilst the mice are running away.
The bird swoops down, grabs a mouse,
And drifts off to his nest.

Rhodri Morgan (10)
Llangan Primary School

The Key To The Sea

As the waves roll in and the tide gets high,
As the seagulls fly beneath the blue, blue sky,
As the mermaids swim through the stormy sea,
On the golden sand there lays a key,
The key to the sea,
The key is made from stories of old,
It's made from secrets never told,
And when somebody finds the key,
They'll take its place and the key will be free.

Alexandra Evans (11)
Llangan Primary School

Wales

They think that Wales is full of hills
That the wind is cold and full of chills,
That there's hundreds of valleys and lots of pits
They think we're a load of silly Welsh twits,
I know that Wales is not a pong,
It's a lovely place and it's full of song.
It's lovely countryside all lovely and green,
Someone should tell them it ought to be seen.

Maxwell Rosser (11)
Llangan Primary School

Summer Roses

Summer roses are so sweet,
Summer roses aren't good to eat.

Summer roses everywhere,
Summer roses in the air,
Summer roses all about,
Summer roses in the field,
Summer roses are so sweet.

Hannah Avery (9)
Llangan Primary School

Kitty Kat

K itty, kitty, clever little kitty
I ngenious little kitty is.
T he cleverest cat in all the world,
T the cleverest cat kitty is!
Y ellow is the colour of little kitty,

K itty is the colour of yellow.
A nd best of all, little kitty is,
T he cleverest cat in the meadow!

Taylor Still (10)
Llangan Primary School

Shadow

Silent in the night a shadow moves,
As quick as a black knight.
Breathing like a diver's last breath,
Limping like a soldier's death,
Dark as the darkest corner in your house,
You can't see his face just like the invisible man.

David Handley (10)
Llangan Primary School

The End

The end is red,
The end is silver.
The end I use to protect,
The end I use to poke,
The end I use for fun.
The end I use to fight,
The end I use to save.
The end is my friend and
My friend is the sword.

George Hawksworth (10)
Llangan Primary School

I Wish

I wish that I could have a brown, silky, funny, playful dog.

I wish war could end. No more guns. No chemicals to kill.

I wish the NSPCC could help more children begging
for nicer parents.

I wish there were more friendly people in the world.

I wish I could feed Africa and give children there a proper life.

I wish I had mountains of shiny pound coins to buy
everything I have wished for.

Ellie Rice (7)
Oldcastle Junior School

The Magic Box

(Based on 'Magic Box' by Kit Wright)

I will put in the box . . .
an elf's hat, filled with mischief,
fire from a flaming inferno in the depths of an erupting volcano,
the horn of the ferocious Minotaur.

I will put in the box . . . .
an Eskimo's boot from an exciting expedition to the Antarctic,
a worthless diamond,
a circular star in a sunny summer's sky.

I will put in the box . . .
three grains of sand from a Hawaiian beach,
the last flight of a falling falcon,
and the first sight of a blind man.

I will put in the box . . .
a swimming hawk and a flying whale,
a wizard on a SAS training course,
and a soldier on a magic carpet.

My box is made from ice,
and is coated in eagle feathers,
its hinges are the talons of an owl.

I shall glide in my box
high above the towering Himalayas
then land in the lush green leaves
of the Amazon rainforest.

Ieuan Loughran (11)
Oldcastle Junior School

Hiding

Where you hide
In a dark, damp cave, blocked with long grass, *waving* swiftly,
Where you hide
Lonely, shivering, curled in a ball of thick fur,

Where you hide
Poachers with vans shimmer in the blurred distance,
Tribes of women walk proudly by,
Hyenas sprint past, flattening the grass.

Where you hide
In your dark, gloomy cave frightened with fear,
Your heart slowly beat as you
Remember sad times,
Your eyes fill up with tears, thinking of death.

The glowing sun sets.
The trees softly blow in the cold breeze, swaying softly like a
rocking cradle.

Where you hide
Footsteps stamp, nearer, louder.
You look up with fright, a long gun is staring fiercely at you,
Bang!

Bethan Sian Hocking (10)
Oldcastle Junior School

Wales

A castle of grey rock
Stands on a hillside,
Still, proud and strong,
Weathering the decay of time.

The long-lost cry of a warrior king
Who took back his nation's land.
Legends lingering in the valleys,
Their heroes' voices whispering from waterfalls.

Snow-topped mountains shrouded in mist,
The murky expanses of tunnels beneath,
No longer mined for their treasures.

The patron, St David, water drinker,
Who lived a life without luxuries,
The preacher who blessed both
People and their land.

Fields of yellow daffodils,
Hills of greenest grass,
Jagged cliffs and massive mountains.

The Welsh, still fighting the English foe,
Roaring in triumph
As the winger scores a try!

The land of an ancient language
That still lives on,
Remaining in the hillsides,
Surviving the centuries.

A raised flag, lifted by the breeze,
Its proud dragon stands defiant
Against any enemy who would
Threaten this proud land.

William Thomas (11)
Oldcastle Junior School

Wales

Hills scarred with sleepy sheep,
Deserted castles where battles were victorious.
The last breath of Caradog
And the first look of Llywelyn.

Lush, light, lovely leeks fill the towns,
Muddy mines black with everlasting tracks.
A mucky miner scribbling away
And a poet collecting coal.

Rain on slate roofs of colourful terraced houses,
A fearless pony and a silent choir.
Rushing rivers flow to the slippery stepping stones,
While St David's daffodils bloom.
Rebecca rioters resting, waiting for the night,
The land of the everlasting language
And the restless rugby team winning their games.
Brave warriors battle their way to the top,
Congregations attend the caring chapel.

A gorgeous, golden harp playing beautifully
To a scarlet fire-breathing dragon.

Mountains covered in wintry, white snow,
St Dwynwen sending out love.
Peaceful countryside, great for relaxing,
Farms filled with friendly animals.

The Welsh flag fluttering over the peaceful towns,
St David rising ready to preach.
Sandy, soft beaches delighting people at the shore,
The sound of cheers from the Millennium stadium in Cardiff,
The capital city.

A warm welcome from Wales - croeso!

Catherine Felton (11)
Oldcastle Junior School

The Magic Box

(Based on 'Magic Box' by Kit Wright)

I will put in my box . . .
a locket made from gems,
fire from a fairy-tale dragon,
the eclipse from the year 2000 that nobody saw.

I will put in my box . . .
a butterfly made from diamonds,
a glove made of raindrops,
a mini statue that tribes used to worship,
a butterfly clip made from crystals,
given to me on a bride's wedding day.

I will put in my box . . .
the memory of when I sat on the rings of Saturn,
three sad memories that I'll never forget,
the last breath of my dying hamster,
and the first smile I ever saw when I was born.

I will put in my box . . .
a purple ocean,
a cat on a skateboard,
and a boy on a mouse hunt.

My box is fashioned from silk and gold and silver,
with feathers on the lid and memories in the corners.
It's hinges are some pieces from the moon.

I shall glide in my box
with all the birds flying south,
then land on a sand dune in the Sahara Desert.

Hayley Norris (11)
Oldcastle Junior School

The Sea

The sea is a charging rhinoceros
She's brutal and grey
She stampedes into rocks all day
Her sharp horns and ferocious bite
She's rapidly snorting.

The sea is a slow turtle
Tiny and turquoise
She swims gracefully all day
Her little eyes staring, she keeps on glaring
She follows everyone.

The sea is a giant dolphin
He's polite and calm
He swims peacefully all day
He has sharp teeth but he does not harm
He's leaping playfully.

The sea is a bloodthirsty anaconda
He's violent and vicious
He chomps the rocks all day
With his sharp teeth and he bites galore
He slithers to his prey.

Ceri-Anne Thomas (9)
Oldcastle Junior School

Hiding

Where you hide
In a rotting rabbit hole
Where you hide
Laying down poking your head out with fear
Where you hide
You see a sneaking, slithering snake eating what is left of the rabbit
You see cheetahs slaughtering antelope, you think you are next
Where you hide in your terrifying world of everlasting darkness
                                                    and hunger
You're lonely and frightened, you feel threatened
You're horrified, shivering with fear
A vulture effortlessly swoops and circles you overhead
The blazing hot sun turns your fur a golden brown
Where you hide you hear a gunfire echo in the distance
You are happy to see your mother coming towards you with a
                        delicious antelope hanging from her mouth.

Bethan Jehu (9)
Oldcastle Junior School

I Wish . . .

I wish that I could go to Korea
so I could meet my lovely grandma
and my family.

I wish not a single terrifying war
would happen ever again.

I wish everyone could live
with fresh water to drink.

I wish that everyone would listen
to God and read the Bible.

I wish that all these wishes
would come true.

Byoung-In Min (8)
Oldcastle Junior School

Hiding

Where you hide
    the dead grass silently and smoothly sways all around you.
Where you hide
    your surroundings seem to tremble with terror.
Where you hide
    a hunter steps right over your head towards a figure in the
    distance while elephants and rhinos stampede wildly into
    the deep horizon.
Where you hide
    in your world of absolute hunger, all alone, your fear of death
    is now much stronger than normal. Your mouth feels like the
    waterhole near your den. The sun burns more intensely than
    ever before. The heat of the savannah is stronger than usual.
Where you hide
    you hear a distant gunshot, and a thump as something falls.
You dart over to the spot, only to find your mother motionless on
    the ground.

Daniel Catton (9)
Oldcastle Junior School

I Wish

I wish that I could talk to animals all over the world and be their friend and stop everyone from killing them.

I wish Adam and Ben to have a nice happy birthday with their presents and birthday cards.

I wish that we had more snow in this country so everyone could build snowmen and have snow fights.

I wish that nobody in the world had an argument ever, because it feels horrible to have one.

I wish that my next-door neighbour's friend would come home from hospital so I could see her again.

Rachael Sparrow (7)
Oldcastle Junior School

Hiding

Where you hide
 In a dark ditch in the ground
Where you hide
 Curled up waiting you're scared and lonely.

Where you hide
 You see a rhino charging towards you,
 You see the hunter's boots shining in the grass,
 You see elephants stomping down the grass.

Where you hide
 In your place of fear
 Your home is dark, you're terrified,
 You're scared and hungry waiting for food,
 A vulture glides above you,
 The sun shines in your glimmering eyes.

Where you hide
 You hear a gunshot
 You feel a scratch on your stomach, your mother's back.

Josh Harris (9)
Oldcastle Junior School

I Wish . . .

I wish I could rule the universe
and have such strong, mighty power.

I wish that there were world peace
so there would be no war.

I wish that I could stop world hunger
so no one would ever starve.

I wish that I could cure all illnesses
so no one would ever be ill.

I wish that I could fly and see the
tiny blue world below.

Morgan Neagle (7)
Oldcastle Junior School

Hiding

Where you hide
    In the long, swaying, sloping, smooth grass in the shade of a tree.

Where you hide
    A snake slithers by.
    You see hyenas circling a dying antelope, you cry in fear.
    An eagle swoops down swiftly for its prey.

Where you hide
    In your threatened world,
    You're dehydrating, you're close to death.
    You're terrified without your mother.
    A vulture circles you waiting for death.
    The stars twinkle for the last time.

Where you hide
    You hear a gunshot then laughter.
    You look around then you feel something hard.
    You feel like you're in a world of darkness and on your own.

Amy Roberts (9)
Oldcastle Junior School

I Wish . . .

I wish I were a speeding Great Dane
and run like the rushing wind.

I wish I could be a brave diver
and meet a ferocious shark.

I wish I were a scuttling ant
and dig deep dark, hollow holes.

I wish I lived in a wonderful Legoland
and enjoyed the zooming rides.

I wish I could live in the murky underwater
and make my home in a rotting shipwreck.

I wish I could eat chewy sweets all day
and break the 'most plump person' record.

Charlotte Barrett (8)
Oldcastle Junior School

Hiding

Where you hide
    In the golden corn fields camouflaged
Where you hide
    Lying down like nothing is bothering you.

Where you hide
    There are slithering snakes weaving
    Through the dry grasslands and zebras
    Galloping away from hunters.

Where you hide
    In your terrified and hungry world
    Your open field of lush swaying corn
    Your dried up mouth dying of thirst

    An owl staring at you furiously
    The vultures are circling you

Where you hide
    You hear a gunshot in the distance
    You hear whispering hunters then *bang!*

Nathan Jones (10)
Oldcastle Junior School

I Wish . . .

I wish that the world were made of snow so that we could
always play in the snow.

I wish that Africa could have rain so they could have a proper life.

I wish that world wars would stop so that people would not die.

I wish that I had thirty million pounds so I could buy anything.

I wish that everyone could stay alive and no one would die.

I wish that I had never-ending chocolate so that I could
always eat it.

I wish that Africa would become normal so that they would
be happy.

Adam Davies (8)
Oldcastle Junior School

The Sea

The sea is a ferocious lion
Thrashing and crashing, killing his prey
He drags in everything in reach all day
With his shiny claws and jagged jaws ready to pounce
He prowls the sand, everyone's his enemy.

At night the sea is still a lion yet there's something different about him
He's bored and tired but you won't hear a snore
He lies on his back stretching his shiny claws
With his eyes glowing gazing in stillness
He stares at the beach, everyone's his enemy.

The sea is still a lion, but he is changed again
He paddles and splashes in the warm water
He gives the occasional splash to passers-by
He watches the bay, everyone's his friend.

Elinor Thomas (8)
Oldcastle Junior School

The Sea

The sea is a speedy cheetah rushing up and down the beach.
Up and down that soggy beach it whizzes all day long.
Its tail really whips and slams,
Against those rocks that look like dams.

The sea is a great big alligator snapping and biting at the
small, helpless rocks.
On his calm days in July and August, he lies and basks over the
beach all day.
With his sharp teeth sparkling and glinting in the bright midday sun.

The sea is a swift, quick lizard that rapidly makes its way
down the saturated beach.
On calm days it crawls down the dunes all day,
But then, unexpectedly, it makes a brief noise,
A lizard noise, 'Slurp, slurp!'

Charles Cottrell (9)
Oldcastle Junior School

Hiding

Where you hide
In a sharp, prickly bush resting, resting
Where you hide
Curled up in a petrified ball and shaking.

Where you hide
Hyenas stalk past searching for you,
Poachers come and go past your hiding place,
In the distance a shimmering lake shines brightly in the sun.

Where you hide
In your mind you try to fight fear,
Your brown eyes water, thinking of death,
Your heart beats slowly, sadly missing love.

A blue shadow of a buzzard flies on the ground around you,
The sun glares down cooking you in your skin,
Where you hide
You hear the bang of a silver gun!
You see your world fading away.

Hollie Morgan (9)
Oldcastle Junior School

Hiding

Where you hide
Up in your silent treetop.

Where you hide
The leaves turn to ashes.

Where you hide
The orange flames blow you
Animals run in every direction
Fleeing for their lives.

Where you hide
In your burning stronghold,
Your slowing heartbeat tells you you will die
Your mind says you will not.

A buzzard darts at a burnt mouse but is engulfed by flame
The sun is destroying the land.

Where you hide
You hear flames creep up on you
You feel your fur burning, you know this is the end.

Tomas Morgan (9)
Oldcastle Junior School

Hiding

Where you hide
   Moonlight grass sweeps around you
Where you hide
   The rustle of leaves tickles your feet.

Where you hide
   The sound of snakes slithering their way towards you while
   The elephants storm loudly through the slippery mud
   The echo of crickets scares you stiff.

Where you hide
   In your lonely world feeling worried and scared
   Your heart is pounding, you feel hungry and thirsty
   Your mouth feels dry and you know you're
   Alone.

   A vulture rapidly flies as he gleams in the
   Glittering moon
   The stars you see shining above you.

Where you hide
   You hear a gunshot that makes you shake
   You see a hunter's body as you fall to the ground.

Martha Parrish (10)
Oldcastle Junior School

Hiding

Where you hide
   In the dry, dark grass craving thirst.
Where you hide
   In the gloomy, uninteresting grassland tiredly dragging
   yourself.

Where you hide
   A pack of vultures hurtling towards a dead zebra
   And a pride of lions go to an unwary buffalo to devour
   its flesh.

Where you hide
   In your world of hunger and despair
   Your moaning growls filled with sadness and hunger.
   Your terrified, quivering heart pounding like a drum.

   A raging cheetah eagerly chasing a gazelle
   The sun intensifies the heat of the desert.

Where you hide
   You hear the cries of a dying animal
   You see your mother, but she is painted in red and
   motionless.

Huw Lewis (9)
Oldcastle Junior School

Hiding

Where you hide,
In a spiky, poisonous bush.
Where you hide,
Petrified and lonely, curled up in a shaking ball.
Where you hide,
Laughing hyenas prowl with a watchful eye,
Warriors with spears looking for fresh meat,
Poachers looking for animal heads, ivory and skins.
Where you hide,
In your blood-covered ball of fur fearful for your life
Your heart beating loudly over all other sounds
You're afraid it will give you away.

A vulgar vulture circles hazardously in the bright sky,
The scorching sun cooks you alive, your frightened body boiling
Where you hide
You hear the terrifying war cry of tribal warriors
You turn around and are deafened by gunshot,
Your life flashes before your eyes.

Reuben Fisher (10)
Oldcastle Junior School

Hiding

Where you hide
    In a sharp, prickly bush.
Where you hide
    Curled in a ball, terrified while the raging wind blows.

Where you hide
    Vultures surround you
    You see their deadly shadows
    A stampede rages over the horizon
    Hyenas laugh at you with their gloomy eyes.

Where you hide
    In your thick coat of fur
    You howl in the moonlight
    Your heart beats like an eagle swooping down for its prey
    A small tear falls as you think of your family
    A buzzard stares at you weeping
    The sun blinds your eyes.

Where you hide
    You hear horrifying footsteps approaching
    You see a loaded gun barrel in your face.

Lewis Down (9)
Oldcastle Junior School

The Sea

The sea is a smooth cat
Calm and gentle.
It silently sleeps all day.
With his curvy head between his furry paws,
He snores quietly through the starry night.

The sea is a grey rat
Large and hairy.
It moves loudly all day.
With his glowing eyes,
He scampers all day.

The sea is a growling lion
Fierce and deafening.
It hunts wildly for prey all day.
With his furry mane swishing in the moonlight,
He is frisky and dangerous.

The sea is a slippery snake
Sliding and splashing in the breeze.
It makes a rattling noise.
With his tail waving menacingly all day
He is scary.

Kate Jones (8)
Oldcastle Junior School

Hiding

Where you hide
    In a prickly, thorny bush in the savannah.

Where you hide
    You're curled up achy, lonely and worried.

Where you hide
    Hyenas in the far distance race after their prey.
    A huge stampede of wildebeest, run as far as the wind,
    Straight past your hiding place.

Where you hide
    In your furry coat, shaking like an earthquake,
    Your heart beats in sorrow,
    You remember your happy days with pride.

    A vulture circles you leaving a deadly shadow,
    The sunset fades in the distance.

Where you hide
    You hear a man's soft footprint,
    You take your last breath, you see darkness.

Jessie Rebecca Hathaway (9)
Oldcastle Junior School

Wales

Rain patters instantly on grey slate rooftops,
The wind whistles as the daffodils wave to and fro,
Sheep's fleeces frizz in the bitter, misty air.

Old folk sit by a cosy, open fire in a venerable cottage,
Eating Welsh cakes, sweet and tasty,
Reciting poetry by famous poets.

Sun shines brightly over muddy mountains,
Daffodils sway in the early morning breeze,
And lambs leap and jump in the glistening green grass,
Welsh folk dancers sing and dance beautifully as the day goes by.

Meanwhile . . .
A raging, red, fire-breathing dragon,
Sleeps in an old crammy cave waiting for nothing else,
Daffodils stop swaying, lambs stop leaping,
There's nothing else to do but wait.

Kate Manning (10)
Oldcastle Junior School

I Wish . . .

I wish I were a dazzling star,
So that I could look over the beautiful world.

I wish I could be a bloodthirsty dragon,
So that I could swoop over the frosty hilltops.

I wish I could be a glistening bird,
So that I could flutter in the midnight sky,

I wish I were a sparkling pot of gold,
So that someone could come and snatch me.

I wish I could be a smiling sunflower in a grassy field,
So that I could wave gracefully in the warm wind.

I wish I could be a scar-faced pirate,
So that I could dart at people with my razor-sharp sword.

Amy Sandford (8)
Oldcastle Junior School

The Sea

The sea is a ferocious cheetah
Lashing against the jagged rocks.
It dangerously pounces on its helpless prey all day,
With its frothy mouth and sharp teeth,
It attacks the creatures down beneath.

The sea is a pretty dolphin.
Jumpy and a gleaming silver.
She gracefully leaps all day,
With her smallish fins.
She rapidly swims
Underneath the turquoise.

The sea is a crazy monkey,
Swiftly moving, always on the go.
He bounds all day long,
With his long, swervy tail.
He leaps above the heavy rocks.

Conor Lynn (9)
Oldcastle Junior School

I Wish . . .

I wish I were a zooming aeroplane
gliding above the glistening seas.

I wish I were an everlasting, delicious chocolate bar
filled with crunchy nuts and sticky caramel.

I wish I were a ferocious orange and black tiger
pouncing in the long, smooth grass.

I wish I were a golden monkey
swinging across the green silky vines.

I wish I were a whizzing rocket
blasting across the shiny Milky Way.

I wish I were a gleaming red sports car
zooming across the hot, steamy jungle.

Adam Brown (7)
Oldcastle Junior School

Wales

Dainty daffodils dancing in the dew,
Bright and yellow, standing tall.
Lush leeks lazing in the lawn,
Attractive and green waving to and fro very slowly.

The spirited ancient castle,
Still strong and standing.
Memories of bloody battles
Joyfully won.

Singing and dancing merrily
Around warm camp fires,
Reciting poetry from famous poets
And hearing angry roars from dragons at the misty mountain.

Memories from great victories
At rugby matches or cricket.
Enormous cheers from the Millennium Stadium.
National Anthem sung.

Nia Williams (10)
Oldcastle Junior School

I Wish . . .

I wish I were a golden eagle
swooping and swirling over the snowy mountains.

I wish I were a zooming racing car
swishing down the racing track.

I wish I were a dazzling princess
who rules the cool world.

I wish I were a fire-breathing dragon
frightening and scaring people away.

I wish I were a lazy farm cat
sleeping in a cool barn.

I wish we could have snow every day
so I could throw whizzing snowballs.

Bethan Mason (8)
Oldcastle Junior School

Wales

King Arthur and Merlin arouse the mighty dragon,
Then the dragon wins them many battles
To protect the pride of Wales,
King Arthur now in his grave, waiting to be summoned.

The rain falls heavily into the fields.
The sheep graze in fields,
Where the leeks and daffodils grow,
And springs and rivers flow.

People dancing joyfully,
Singing the National Anthem,
The Eisteddfod is coming,
Folk dancing on the day.

The Millennium Stadium standing mightily
Wales play rugby inside,
JPR Williams makes it 5-0 to the Welsh.
The Welsh flag standing proud.

Ryan Stacey (10)
Oldcastle Junior School

Wales

The windy and wet wintry weather
Dripping down the drains,
The cold sheep are shivering on the frosty mountains.

The muddy mines are filled up with glittering black gold,
Remember to huddle up in the corner away from the cold.

The castle stands there so tall and proud,
The battle's coming closer 'cause it's getting terribly loud.

The daily daffodils are dancing in the dew
The long leeks are laughing as the dragon runs off in fright,
The children are going to sleep now
As their parents say, 'Night-night.'

Lois John (10)
Oldcastle Junior School

I Wish . . .

I wish I were a prickly maze
with swervy turns and dazzling green hedges

I wish I were a ginger cat
to prowl in the sparkly night

I wish I were a sly shark
with jaws as sharp as glistening razors

I wish I were a silky horse
whizzing through a rapid race

I wish I were a rainbow flower
swaying in the summer breeze

I wish I were the famous Queen Elizabeth
with glowing skin and a golden crown.

Ellie Jane Morgan (8)
Oldcastle Junior School

I Wish . . .

I wish to be mysteriously magical and make people
happy and laugh.

I wish to please everyone and to give food to Africa
so that they have happy lives.

I wish to make all poor people have food and
proper homes.

I wish for people on the streets to survive cold weather.

I wish to go to Santa's workshop and see Rudolph and fly over
the cold, shimmering moon and see the perfect sparkling stars.

I wish nasty hunters to stop killing innocent animals.

I wish to be famous and sing live on stage.

I wish my auntie and uncle to get back together.

Alys Clark (8)
Oldcastle Junior School

A Poem To Be Spoken Silently

It was so quiet that I heard the clock ticking.

It was so quiet that I heard the teacher's skirt
rustling as she worked.

It was so quiet that I heard the petals
of the sunflower opening.

It was so quiet that I heard the sand falling
through the egg timer.

Ian Richards   (9)
Pencoed Junior School

A Poem To Be Spoken Silently

It was so quiet that I hard a bat flapping its wings.

It was so quiet that I heard a sweet wrapper blowing
across the pavement.

It was so quiet that I heard a rat under my bed.

It was so quiet that I heard a spider in my room,
on the wall in the corner.

Susan James   (10)
Pencoed Junior School

A Poem To Be Spoken Silently

It was so quiet that I heard people breathing
as they slept.

It was so quiet that I heard myself groaning
in the night.

It was so quiet that I heard the moon saying
'Goodnight'.

It was so quiet that I heard the squeaking
of the pen on the whiteboard.

Ieuan Parrish   (9)
Pencoed Junior School

Just Me

Sometimes I think
There's just me in the whole world.

Who else knows
What I am doing?

Who else knows
About me in my bedroom?

Who else knows
The games I have?

Who else knows
How awful it is
Not to be able to skip?

Who else knows
That I'm trying my best to work?

Nobody knows except me
And I'm the only one of me
In the whole wide world.

Ricky Elward (9)
Pencoed Junior School

Just Me

Sometimes I think
There's just me
In the whole world,

Who else knows what I dream about in my bed at night?
Who else knows where the little planet people walk?
Who else knows how awful it is to be called names?
Who else knows how to get to Level 5 on my XBox
James Bond game?

Nobody knows except me
And I'm the only one of me
In the whole wide world.

Leum Williams (9)
Pencoed Junior School

My Family

Everyone in my family is different,
Me, my mum, my dad and my sister,
My sister Chloe loves eating sweets,
And thinks my dad has very smelly feet,
My mum loves cooking spaghetti Bolognese,
Everyone that tries it seems very amazed,
My dad likes football and rugby too,
And also likes telling other people what to do,
My cousins are very, very nice,
One of them can't stop eating rice,
My family has lots of pets,
Who sometimes need to go to the vet's,
My best friend is Cerys,
But she's nothing like Dennis the Menace,
I like my family from head to toe,
So there is something you should know,
This is the end of my poem.

Sophie Thompson (9)
Pencoed Junior School

Just Me

Sometimes I think there's just me in the whole world.

Who else knows what I think about at night?
Who else knows about the elves speaking
in the tree trunks?
Who else knows the trees speak to the flowers
in the night and in the morning?
Who else knows how awful it is when people
pick on my friends?
Who else knows that the tigers are playing
with their cubs?

Nobody knows except me and I'm the only one
of me in the whole wide world.

Luke Phillips (11)
Pencoed Junior School

Games Galore!

Roller hockey's great mate, see the puck,
Whack it, smack it,
Football is such fun and glory,
But if you're a goalie, that's a different story,
In swimming I used to use a float,
But now I float just like a boat,
Gym is dangerous but keeps you fit,
A leotard and shorts for kit,
Rugby's rough, I think it's for boys,
So girls, just stick with Barbie toys,
Chess is quite a boring game,
But I sometimes play it, all the same,
Netball is fun but can be hard,
The talent, you can't buy with a credit card,
But for now, it's the weekend,
So games won't drive me round the bend,
I'll watch TV and eat some sweets,
I'll raid the cupboard of all the treats,
Then I'll sit down and have a snore,
But then tomorrow, it's games galore!

Phillipa Lauren Smith (11)
Pencoed Junior School

A Poem To Be Spoken Silently

It was so quiet that I heard a bat
flapping its wings in the darkness of the night.

It was so quiet that I heard a creak on my door
as it opened in the wind.

It was so quiet that I heard a vampire in my
cupboard as I lay in bed.

It was so quiet that I heard a cat sitting down
outside my window.

Hannah James (11)
Pencoed Junior School

Behind The Cute

Behind the cute the cats are planning,
Always planning, always waiting,
It's almost time for the world,
To get what it deserves.

It's a privilege, not a punishment,
Always planning, always waiting,
Soon the cats will rule the world,
Soon, soon, soon, soon.

Behind the cute are brilliant minds,
Scheming, planning, holding meetings,
Soon the cats will rule the world,
Soon, soon, soon, soon.

It's not for evil, just for power,
They'll treat the humans well, and fair,
They'll solve the world's problems,
Soon, soon, soon, soon.

They'll always be loving,
And purr when you stroke them,
They'll always comfort you,
Always be there for you,
Always, always, always, always.

Always planning, always waiting,
Waiting for the right time,
Waiting for their destiny.

Cerys Hoskins (11)
Pencoed Junior School

A Poem To Be Spoken Silently

It was so quiet that I heard the sea whisper at the shore.
It was so quiet that I heard the sun say, 'Good morning!'
It was so quiet that I heard the animals making homes
                                    under the sand.
It was so quiet that I heard the sea creatures whispering.

Whitney Brown (10)
Pencoed Junior School

Friends

Friends are great to be with,
My friends are Sophie, Cerys, Hayley, Shauna,
Molly-Ann, Rebecca, Molly and Jessica.

Sophie is great to be with,
She is funny, sometimes silly.
Cerys is great to be with,
She likes to have fun.
Hayley is great to be with
She is really funny and really silly
And she makes people laugh.
Shauna is nice to be with,
She is sometimes mad.
Rebecca is nice to be with,
She is sometimes mad.
Molly-Ann is great to be with,
She has a great singing voice
And is sometimes silly.
Molly is nice to be with,
She is very quiet all the time.
Jessica is nice to be with,
She is really mad sometimes.
And they are all my friends.

Rhian Simmonds (10)
Pencoed Junior School

A Poem To Be Spoken Silently

It was so quiet that I heard sand falling
through an egg timer.

It was so quiet that I heard people breathing.

It was so quiet that I heard the clock ticking.

It was so quiet that I heard lights humming
in the classroom.

Scott Henwood (9)
Pencoed Junior School

The Poor Tiger

Among the trees, something's stirring,
A yawn, a stretch and the loudest of purring,
As the sun sets the tiger prowls,
And in the distance, hyenas howl,
Creeping through the long grass to hunt his prey,
Still many hours till the break of day,
The tiger hunts alone, and mainly at night,
Using his keen senses, especially his sight,
He spots his victim and stands perfectly still,
Getting ready to attack, getting ready to kill,
He moves cautiously forward, his meal is in sight,
The deer raises its head, it's too late for the flight,
The tiger charges, slashing his cruel claws,
The deer is grounded as the tiger snaps his jaws,
With his belly full, it's time for him to rest,
All of the tiger skills have been put to the test,
The tiger's struggle for survival is over for the night,
But as the dawn chorus begins, he faces a new fight,
This powerful beast, with a coat so stripy and sleek,
Is hunted illegally by man, so his future looks bleak,
His ground-up bones heal sick people, they say,
They have mysterious powers, keep the flu at bay,
These supreme hunters are becoming extinct without a doubt,
So illegal poachers have got to be wiped out.

Jobe Aaron Parrish (10)
Pencoed Junior School

A Poem To Be Spoken Silently

It was so quiet that I heard the sand
falling through an egg timer.

It was so quiet that I heard the wind
whisper before the storm.

It was so quiet that I heard the floorboards
talk to the walls.

Samantha Johns (11)
Pencoed Junior School

Playtime

Playtime is fun,
But sometimes boring.
Out in the sun
Or the cold.
Whatever the weather, it's fun,
Forever and ever it is.

Sometimes it's raining,
Sometimes it's not.
But I like it sunny,
And sometimes wet.
But whatever the weather, it's fun.

I wish it could last forever,
And a day,
But the whistle blows.
Then a crash and a thud,
To run to lines,
And everyone's back to their classes.

Samantha McLaren-Brown (9)
Pencoed Junior School

Colours Of The World

If the world didn't have colours
Oh what would we do?
Our life would be gloomy
No green, red or blue.

The grass would be black
The skies would be grey
I'm glad we are living
In colour today.

So let us be grateful
For what we have got
There's not one sign of darkness
'Cause we've got the lot.

Louise Howard (9)
Pencoed Junior School

My Dog Bengie

Bengie is a dog
He likes to chew a log

He lies in bed
And he scratches his head

He plays with me
And barks at me

He jumps up and down
And chews his play crown

He eats my book
Then takes a look

He bites my toes
And licks my clothes

Apart from that he is my dog
And I will always love him.

Lauren Cox (10)
Pencoed Junior School

Legends

Legends are fun,
Legends are true,
Legends, legends, are fun to read.

Beasts and heroes,
You will find in legends.
Legends, legends, are fun to read.

The death of the beast,
And the hero filled with joy.
Legends, legends, are fun to read.

When the beast is dead,
The people are happy.
Legends, legends are fun to read.

Alex Rice (9)
Pencoed Junior School

Am I Going Crazy?

I was walking down the street,
With an ice cream taller than the trees,
I found an elf,
Who had a big mouth,
So I flushed him down the loo
He got covered in . . . phew!
Got into the sewer then . . .
He turned bluer
He came back through the tap
And sat on my lap
I took him to the park
He got taken away by a lark
So I went home
He rang the phone
Then I went to the door
He was lying on the floor
I sent him to Mars
He gave me some bars
My mum had a baby
Am I going crazy?

Holly McHugh (10)
Pencoed Junior School

My Dad's POV

He hates hugs and kisses,
Unless they are from the missus
He drives a family Megane
Unless he gets a Sedan.
He wants a jeep,
The type that goes *beep!*
He likes his sleep
Unless his jeep goes *beep!*
That's my dad's POV!

Dominic Luff (10)
Pencoed Junior School

My Mum

She is sweet
She gives me treats
I love her and she loves me.

She makes me happy when I'm down
Her face never ever has a frown.

My brother sometimes has a mood
But my mum makes us lovely food.

I always forgive her if she shouts at me
She takes us out, yes, all us three.

Sometimes she is really funny
She buys me clothes with her money.

I'm glad I've got her, really I am
I love her and that is true.

Jessica Brown (9)
Pencoed Junior School

My Dog Jessie

Jess is a dog
She likes to chew a sock
She lies in her bed
And then she scratches her head
She plays with her bone
She lies on me
She bites me
She rips up shoes
She jumps off a wall and lands on the ground
She chases our cat
Jess is the best dog of all.

Jack Hiscocks (10)
Pencoed Junior School

Three Of My Friends

Sophie is my best friend
She makes me laugh a lot
But when we start laughing
We just can't stop.

Then there's Hayley Selway
She's really, really funny
She makes me smile all the time
Even when it's sunny.

Rhian Simmonds is a great friend
She sometimes makes me smile
But sometimes she gets serious
And goes a little funny for a while.

Cerys Thomas (10)
Pencoed Junior School

My Friends

My friends are all funny
They make me laugh
Sophie is the laugher
Rhian is the smiler.
I like Cerys too
She helps me in the things I do.
Molly-Ann is the singer and very polite too
And my bestest friend as well.
Jessie is sometimes quiet, sometimes not
But Molly Jenkins is the quietest of the lot.
Rebecca always talks to us, she is funny too
Shauna plays footie, Danielle too.
But Danielle is different, she is a tomboy too
But I am just average and I hope they like me too.

Hayley Selway (10)
Pencoed Junior School

My Crazy Friends

My friends are crazy
They mess around in school
They act like little monkeys
They think the teacher's cool!

They think the headmaster's fantastic
They think school dinners are yummy
But when I eat school dinners
There's a horrible feeling in my tummy.

They like uniforms
They don't take baths
I don't know what's wrong with them
They even like maths!

They always tidy up
They're not a bit lazy
But this is what I think about my friends
I think they're crazy!

Rebecca Baker (11)
Pencoed Junior School

Flower Power

My mum likes tulips
With all the bright red tips
They're her favourite flowers
They give her special powers
She loves them lots.
She puts them in tulip pots.

Ross Hall (10)
Pencoed Junior School

Thierry Henry

Thierry Henry is my idol and always will be,
Henry on the ball, he should curl it but will he?
He curls it into the goal and shouts to the crowd.

Henry plays for Arsenal,
Who are the third best team in the world
Sometimes he makes an obvious dive and hurls himself.

Henry plays for France who are a very good team
He plays alongside Wiltord and Pires.

I love the way he glides with the ball
He drives me crazy,
He's really cool.

But what I'm wondering is why
Manchester United don't buy him
Because I support *Man U!*

Joseph Housley (11)
Pencoed Junior School

Hannah

My sister Hannah is the best
She's always putting me to the test
She sees who's first eating breakfast in the morning
She makes me stay up late so I'm always yawning
She slams her door with a big loud *boom!*
She's always telling me, 'Get out of my room!'
Apart from all that she is my sister
When she goes away I always miss her
She snuggles me up when I'm feeling blue
She gives me a hug and says, 'I love you!'

Elinôr Clark (10)
Pencoed Junior School

Poor Family

I know a poor old lady,
It's hard to believe she was once a baby,
She looks a bit like a hag,
And sleeps on a dirty old rag,
Some people feel sorry,
Because all she does is drive a lorry.

I know a poor old man,
He sleeps in a manky old van,
I wish he would go away,
In June, November or May,
He is not very nice,
All he eats is pasta and rice.

I know a poor young girl,
She's never seen a pearl,
She is a bit smelly,
She can't afford a telly,
I think she is sad,
Because she is going mad.

I know a poor young boy,
He's never seen a toy,
He gets upset,
When the weather is wet,
In the middle of May,
He sleeps on hay.

I know you must be asking
What these people have in common,
It's not really a problem,
Telling you,
This is true,
All these four people must be,
A poor family.

Leah Andrews (10)
Pencoed Junior School

The Weather

Sun is a lovely kind of weather,
It gives us lots of light,
It keeps me warm through the day,
Sun is my favourite weather.

Weather is something you can't make,
It happens all so naturally,
You can't control the weather
There's nothing we can do.

Rain is a wet kind of weather,
It will get you soaking,
It can pour and drench you,
Rain is my not-so-favourite weather.

Wind is a horrible kind of weather,
It blows you around,
It blows you so hard
That you might have to leave the ground!

Stormy weather is a type of weather,
Thunder screeches, bangs and crashes,
Lightning blazing, beaming and flashing,
Stormy weather is a type of weather.

Clouds are a kind type of weather,
White and cuddly,
And fluffy and plain,
Clouds are a kind type of weather.

Christian Alex Williams (10)
Pencoed Junior School

Jesus

J esus was born at Christmas time and died at Easter time.
E verybody celebrates His death.
S tories of Him are admired in churches and cathedrals.
U s and everyone believe in Jesus
S un and stars and Earth were created by God.

Ieuan Griffiths (9)
Pencoed Junior School

School

School is fun,
School is cool,
School is like a big, big pool.

If at playtime, it's soaking wet,
Grab a piece of paper and a pen.
Draw a teacher,
Draw a friend,
Draw a dog riding a hen.

But if you're in the playground,
Have a game of tag,
But make sure you don't play football
With someone else's bag!

School is fun,
School is cool,
School is like a big, big pool.

Bleddyn Jury (10)
Pencoed Junior School

Family And Friends And My Pets

Family and friends are very helpful,
And my dogs are very joyful.
Friends are there when you are down,
Or maybe they like to hang around.
My family is very loving
My friends can sometimes be annoying,
But my puppies and dogs are very cute,
And my friends are very nice.
My family gives me gifts,
And I give them a kiss to thank them.
When my dogs play,
I always enjoy watching,
And my family ask me if I've had a nice day.

Kelly Tucker (11)
Pencoed Junior School

Colours Of The Rainbow

Well here we go, let's start from the top,
Red, the colour of a strawberry lollipop.

Orange is next, it's the colour of Sunny Delight,
It's also the colour of a light shining bright.

Yellow is the colour of the shining sun,
It's also the colour of a Danish bun.

Green is the colour of the grass beneath my feet,
It's also the colour of the grapes I love to eat.

Blue is the colour of things when cool,
It's also the colour of my local swimming pool.

Pink is the colour of a smelly old pig,
It's also the colour of a clown's funny wig.

Purple is the colour of a nice juicy plum,
It's also the colour of your thumb when numb.

And all that is left is the pot of gold,
And I get that for the best poem ever told.

Autumn Bevan (11)
Pencoed Junior School

My Cat Molly

My cat Molly
Black as a bat
With a white chest
And paws like a ghost
Likes staying in
And having a hug
She shows she is the best
By sticking out her chest
Yes, that is my cat Molly.

Naomi Jenkins (10)
Pencoed Junior School

I'm Rich

I live in a mansion,
And I'm filled with glee,
I'm happy that I'm rich,
Now let's wait and see.

A year ago, I won the lottery,
And that is one true fact,
With the money I bought lots of chocolate,
And a sweetie shack.

Diamonds and rubies,
I love them all,
BMWs and Bentleys,
Make other ladies drawl.

I want to hear about you,
Now you've heard about me,
I'm still very happy
And filled with glee.

Salimah Jackson (10)
Pencoed Junior School

About Flying

Over the gardens and over the trees,
Flying with the birds and bees.
The wind was tugging at my hair,
And taking me here, there and everywhere.
I flew with an angel up above
And with the bird of peace, a dove.
Listening to the traffic far below,
Making such a wonderful show.
The smell of cooking wafted up,
Borne on the breeze so I could sup.
It was wonderful for me to fly
And be an angel and never die!

Shauna Blake (11)
Pencoed Junior School

The Haunted House

There are witches in the attic
And ghosts are all around.
There are creaky floorboards
And a bright light flashing.
I scream for help!
There's a zombie in the bedroom.
Dead bodies in the corridor,
And a vampire in the toilet.
Frankenstein's watching telly in the living room,
And a headless chef is eating some potatoes.
'It's 11pm!' I scream. 'It's Wednesday,
I've been here for a day!'
My mother opens the door
And I wake up!

Nikki Letitia Morgan (10)
Pencoed Junior School

My Cats And Me

The names of my cats are Holly and Tammy
Whenever they miaow, it means they are hungry
They chase each other every day
And they keep getting in my way
Holly is not very playful now Tammy's come
Tammy is very playful, she attacks everyone
Tammy chases everything like string and wire
Every time she jumps she gets higher and higher
Tammy is a lovely colour
Holly's colour is different
They are always fighting if they're in the same place
They both like meat and plaice.

Hannah-Marie Jenkins (10)
Pencoed Junior School

Late For School

When I was late for school,
My friend said I was cool,
English, maths and history,
I think it was a mystery.

Then it was time for dinner,
In netball I was a winner,
The teacher said to me,
'What do you want to be?'

Assembly time was great,
I sat right next to my mate,
Then it was time for a prayer
The prayer we said was rare.

Then it was time for us to go home,
Wherever we could roam,
School was over
For yet another day,
So see you in the morning
On the way.

Carly Hale (11)
Pencoed Junior School

Giggsy

Ryan Giggs is magic,
He wears a magic boot,
He plays for Man United,
I'm very glad of that.
He scores a lot of goals,
Because he is the best,
He signed for Man United,
And plays for Wales as well.

Thomas James Shakespeare (10)
Pencoed Junior School

My Dog Jack

My dog is grey and black,
His name rhymes with his colour,
He has his own name and address,
Written on his own collar.

His nose is soft and wet,
His paws are smooth and bare,
He lies down and pulls a frown,
He bites and he doesn't even care!

He's cute, fluffy and black,
His name is Jack,
He's my favourite dog,
When he's sitting quietly on the backyard log.

He's tiny, black and grey,
He's always ready to play,
He's so tiny he fits in my sack,
That's my dog Jack.

Natasha John (11)
Pencoed Junior School

My Puppy

My puppy, Rosie, is so nice,
Even though she sometimes bites.
Rosie digs
And gets really dirty
I sometimes thinks she's very naughty.
Rosie's lively
She bounces everywhere,
She goes to sleep on anyone
Rosie is my friend.

Ria Hearne (10)
Pencoed Junior School

School Time

Please don't send me to school,
It's turning everybody into a fool,
School dinners are bad,
They made people mad.
Last week's leftover stew,
Won't be good for you,
Teachers make you tired,
Sometimes you wish they were fired,
Always shouting in your face,
You run away but it becomes a race,
Bullies acting really mean,
It doesn't matter if your favourite colour's
Red or orange or blue or green,
Don't do anything sneaky like undo his lace,
Or he'll rip you a new face,
If you think about it though, it could be worse,
This school could have a curse.

Matthew Alan Coleman (11)
Pencoed Junior School

Pets

I have two kittens
Called Tabby and Tiddles
They play and fight every day
And most of the time
They are hungry and thirsty
They are cute
They go through your tiny legs
And follow you everywhere you go
Tiddles and Tabby are very cute.

Rebecca Jayne Stuckey (10)
Pencoed Junior School

The School From Hell

This is a poem about my school,
Carry on reading it if you think you're so cool,
If you have nightmares then stop reading,
You'd better believe me, I'm on my knees pleading.

When you enter through the gates,
There they are, a whole lot of apes,
Killing each other in the yard,
The teacher signals with a red card.

You go to dinners and what do you know?
The dinner lady's there with a crossbow,
Everyone sliding along the floor,
Then they fall and break their jaw.

So now you've witnessed what my school is,
It's like gone-off milk with a tiny bit of fizz!

Dylan White (10)
Pencoed Junior School

Brambles

My Brambles,
Is a gentle guinea pig,
He's so cute.

My Brambles,
Rushing to his cosy bed,
Nice and warm.

My Brambles,
Loves me and I love him too,
That's Brambles.

Amy Taylor (11)
Pencoed Junior School

The Teachers In My School Think They're Working In A Zoo

The teachers in my school think they're working in a zoo.
Their classroom features many a creature
Here are just a few;

Mr Lea has a chimpanzee,
It leaps about and wiggles.
It pulls his chair and bumps his chair,
And gives us all the giggles.

Mrs Drake has a ten-foot snake,
Inside a case of glass.
When children shout, she lets it out,
To quieten down the class.

Mr Matt has a vampire bat,
With teeth that smile and bite.
When it's time for sums, it shows its gums,
And helps us get them right.

Mrs Rider wears a spider,
Dangling from one ear.
It does no harm, it's meant to charm,
But fills us full of fear.

Mr Breeze keeps jumping fleas,
In a hat on the window sill.
I wonder why his family all cry,
'Please, Sir, we can't sit still.'

But young Miss Sweet, so nice and neat,
Has the best pet there can be.
I hope she has no other pet,
For neat Miss Sweet has me!

Victoria Raymond (10)
Pencoed Junior School

Murphy

My dog's name is Murphy
He's my best ever friend
My mums says he has no brain
He never goes near a drain
He's so much fun I want to tell the world his name
He's blond with curly hair
He's five years old in dog years
That's thirty-five in human years
He's cute and cuddly and fluffy with fur.

I will never leave him
He's so much fun
I don't think he likes cream buns
He really loves chocolate
He's never had a date
He's always there to play with
He loves his bath
He always goes round the bend
I hope this friendship will never end
He's my lifelong loving friend.

Bethan Williams (11)
Pencoed Junior School

My Two Cats

I have two cats called Topsy and Charlie
Charlie's black and fat
Topsy's brown and skinny
They both like a fuss
And play with my tennis balls,
Charlie watches telly,
While Topsy has a nap.
When you fuss them,
They'll purr extremely loud.

Stephen Jones (10)
Pencoed Junior School

School

School is just too long,
It makes me go ping-pong,

The books are too thick,
They make me really sick,

There is a girl in our class called Tara,
Her nickname's Nitty Nora,
She has nits in her hair,
They're *everywhere!*

I am taller than anyone else,
Even than Mrs Nelse,

The lessons are too boring,
Usually half the class is snoring,

School makes me hungry,
It really, really does,
It makes my poor stomach go buzz, buzz,

I wish there was no school,
I really, really do!

Liam Callaghan (11)
Pencoed Junior School

Teachers

T eachers are the best people on Earth.
E ach and every day I learn something.
A nd every lesson is my favourite lesson.
C ompetitions in school are awesome.
H aving something new to learn.
E ach day in school I love.
R eading is learning as well you know
S chool is the best.

Rhiannon Pritchard (11)
Pencoed Junior School

Greedy Dog

This dog will eat anything:
Apple cores, bacon fat
Milk you put out for the cat
He likes the string that ties the roast
And relishes hot buttered toast.
Hide your chocolates, he's a thief
He'll even eat your handkerchief.
Leave some soup without a lid
You'll wish you never did.
And when you think he's full
You'll catch him eating wool.

This dog will eat anything:
Except for mushrooms and dumplings
And what's wrong with those, I wonder?

Christopher Hind (11)
Pencoed Junior School

The Horrible Pogwarts

When I go to school,
I always play in the pool.
The dinner lady gives us last week's salad,
So I put bear traps in her shoes,
A tenth of teachers are kind, all the rest are nasty,
I think the Principal is a robot from Hell,
Because he broke the school bell,
I'm always beaten up by nutters and bullies,
The teachers make the staircases move,
And I put pins on her chair and gunge in her desk,
And that's the reason why,
I hate *school!*

Michael Cotter-Jones (10)
Pencoed Junior School

Seasons Of The Year

Winter is too cold,
So you'd better wrap up warm,
Winter is too cold.

Snow is falling down,
And it's covering the ground,
Snow is falling down.

Soon spring will be here,
And then new lambs will be born,
Soon spring will be here.

Flowers have just bloomed,
Newborn animals are cute,
Flowers have just bloomed.

Summer I enjoy,
Lollipops I adore,
Summer I enjoy.

Now the cold has gone,
We can play in the warm sun,
Now the cold has gone.

The leaves have turned brown,
And soon they'll be falling,
The leaves have turned brown.

Autumn is here,
We can play with conkers,
Autumn is here.

Seasons of the year,
Are what I enjoy the most,
Seasons of the year.

Jodie Maria Parsons (11)
Pencoed Junior School

My School Is Mad

On my first day at school
My brother said I'm cool
So I had a piece of homework
And finished it quickly.

On the second day of school
I made a best friend.
She said, 'Be careful,
Everybody's mad in this school.'
So I went to maths and I went mad.

On the third day of school
I was a bit of a fool
And at playtime I was being bullied
I went into class and my teacher went crazy,
So I ran away from school and my brother went crazy,
So I sat down and waited
By the lamp post.

On the fourth day of school
I fell over a rock and cut my knee.
Then a robber came and shot the heater
But the heater was blowing fire
And I fell off my chair.

On the fifth day of school,
I was having a good day,
Until this boy came and hit me.
At the end of the day I shouted, 'Hooray!'
Because there was no school the next day.

Abigail Emily Fitches (10)
Pencoed Junior School

Gelert And The Wolf

G elert was a charm
E xcellent with wolves
L oads of food for him to eat
E ven a pretty dog
R eally a fierce thing
T here to protect the baby prince.

Annie Slennett (8)
Pen-Y-Fai CW Primary School

Gelert And The Wolf

G elert was a kind dog
E ven when he was born
L oved his family forever
E ven the baby prince
R escued all of his family
T hen killed by his master.

Emma Oakley (7)
Pen-Y-Fai CW Primary School

Gelert

Gelert was a dog
He loved his family
Gelert was brave
Guarding the baby when the family were hunting
The cot was turned over
The prince saw red and killed his own brave dog, Gelert.

Charlotte Price (7)
Pen-Y-Fai CW Primary School

Gelert

G elert was a dog
E ven he could save people
L oved his family and the baby prince
E ven Gelert was the best
R escuing the baby prince when they were out hunting
T he prince killed Gelert and that's where it ended.

Eleri Thomas (7)
Pen-Y-Fai CW Primary School

Gelert The Brave Dog

Gelert loved his family
Gelert was a dog
Gelert was a helpful dog
Who rescued the baby prince.
Gelert killed the wolf
Gelert saved the day
But died in a horrible way.

Dominic Roberts (8)
Pen-Y-Fai CW Primary School

Gelert And The Wolf

G elert was very brave
E ven though he was just a dog
L oved his family so much
E ven though he was a hunter
R escued the child
T here to protect the baby prince.

Nia David (8)
Pen-Y-Fai CW Primary School

Gelert And The Wolf

G elert was a helpful dog
E ven saved the prince's baby
L oved their baby and guarded the baby
E ven adored their baby
R escued the child from danger
T ook care of the baby.

Rhys Pascoe (7)
Pen-Y-Fai CW Primary School

Gelert

G elert was brave
E ven though he was a dog
L oved his family so much
E ven the prince's son
R escued his family when they needed help
T he dog did no harm and got killed.

Ellie Gilhooley (7)
Pen-Y-Fai CW Primary School

Gelert And The Wolf

G elert was a friendly dog
E ven though he was brave
L ooked after the baby prince
E ven though he had blood on him
R eally tried to save the baby
T hen killed by his own master.

Victoria Leyshon (8)
Pen-Y-Fai CW Primary School

Gelert The Hero

G ood helper,
E xciting challenger,
L ovely learner,
E ternal liver,
R espectful obeyer,
T ight puller.

T amed tiger,
H orrid monster,
E xcellent racer.

H airy scenter,
E xtraordinary balancer,
R esponsible giver,
O bsessed hero.

Rhiannon Edwards (10)
Pen-Y-Fai CW Primary School

Prince Llewelyn

P rincess Joan was his wife
R iding on his horse in the forest
I nfant baby left with the nurse
N ow Gelert was his favourite dog
C ourage had he
E mergency, Gelert was missing

L ook for him
L ost was Gelert
E veryone wept
W olves had the baby
E ntered Gelert and saved the baby
L ovely Gelert killed by his best friend
'Y elp' was the word they heard
N ow Gelert is buried in Bedd Gelert.

Alexandra Leyshon (9)
Pen-Y-Fai CW Primary School

Gelert

G alloping to the rescue,
E mergency off to rescue the baby,
L oved by Prince Llewelyn,
E veryone noticed Gelert was missing,
R unning to save the baby,
T he grave still stands with the story inscribed on it.

Francesca Upton (10)
Pen-Y-Fai CW Primary School

Gelert The Saver

Baby saver,
Real good chaser

Stag hunter
Lovely helper

Healthy liver,
Extraordinary vision

Always got the shivers
And will always be a hero.

Myriam Hassan (10)
Pen-Y-Fai CW Primary School

Gelert

G oing through the woods
E mergency, he's missing!
L et's all look for him,
E veryone finds him, his mouth drips with blood
R age the prince has,
T urns to kill the dog, he has his last yelp.

Elinor Thomas (10)
Pen-Y-Fai CW Primary School

Kennings

Baby saver
Stag slayer

Wolf killer
Blood ripper

Best hunter
Fast runner

Scent finder
High cryer

Suspicion maker
Death taker

Clever hound
Master bound.

A: Gelert.

Alexander Franklin (9)
Pen-Y-Fai CW Primary School

Prince Llewelyn

P rincess Joan was his wife
R iding through the forest
I n many different hunts
N ow Gelert was his favourite
C rying was he
E ager Gelert missing

L ost was he
'L et's find him'
E veryone was sad
W ept they did
E ntry by Gelert saves the baby
L lewelyn sighed
Y elping Gelert
N ever unaware.

Laura-Jayne Martin (10)
Pen-Y-Fai CW Primary School

Kennings

Wolf masher
Blood splasher

Baby whining
Dog dying

Llewelyn home
Dog alone

Sword in deep
Baby weeps

Blood over head
Dog dead

Baby saved
Dog in grave.

A: Gelert.

Catrin Stephenson (9)
Pen-Y-Fai CW Primary School

The Saver Who! - Kennings

Blood dripper
Wolf dismisser

Jaw smasher
Bone crasher

Baby saver
Merciful repayer

Teeth gnasher
Wild trasher.

A: Gelert.

Jordon Coombes (10)
Pen-Y-Fai CW Primary School

Gelert's Memory

Blood splasher
Wolf smasher

Baby crying
Nurse lying

Gelert hero
Wolf zero

Prince brave
Baby saved

Prince home
Gelert alone

Gelert dead
Sword through his head.

Hayley Thomas (9)
Pen-Y-Fai CW Primary School

Gelert Kennings

Horse rider
A good smiler

Blood dripper
Wolf ripper

Fear zero
A real hero

A favourite dog
All big and strong

Gelert's alone
They're coming

Gelert dead
Knife through his head.

Claire Rowe (9)
Pen-Y-Fai CW Primary School

Guess Who?

Favourite hound,
Friendship bound.

Life saver,
Good behaviour.

Large claws,
Fast paws.

Prince killed him,
Stabbed in limb.

Wolf crusher,
Bone musher.

Claws slasher,
Fast dasher.

Got a big gravestone,
Like to chew a bone.

A - Gelert.

Samuel McColgan (10)
Pen-Y-Fai CW Primary School

Who Am I?

Baby saver
Wolf slayer

Blood drinker
Flesh eater

Favourite hound
Makes a sound

Very brave
A proud grave.

A - Gelert.

Ryan Williams (9)
Pen-Y-Fai CW Primary School

Gelert

Wolf gnasher
Blood splasher

Life saver
Wolf slayer

Loud crying
Sad dying

Fighting brave
Honourable grave.

Luc Thomas (10)
Pen-Y-Fai CW Primary School

The Iron Man's Revenge

'Come on, let's sabotage the Iron Man'
They marched like a colony of ants
As brave as a lion
Where they went
The Iron Man crept as quiet as a baby lark
He jumped over the homes as high as a jet
Roaming the sky
They came in planes, they swooped like an eagle
Groaning, the Iron Man hid in the sea.

Lewis Jon Campbell (8)
Pen-Y-Fai CW Primary School

The Fatal Night

Hogarth was fishing one fatal night
The eyes of the Iron Man were as bright as light
The giant black body as shiny as a can
The Iron Man's hand was as flat as a flan
There was a *munch, crunch!*
His fingers tight in a fist as a banana bunch
It was the Iron Man chomping a man.

Luke Williams (9)
Pen-Y-Fai CW Primary School

The People Saw The Iron Man

The people so shocked to see
The Iron Man's eyes in the tree
His reflecting green eyes as bright as can be
This Iron Man's body was as bright as the sea
This gigantic, black figure who was as tall as a house
But this little person as small as a mouse
Only the people taller than me could see
The Iron Man's eyes in the tree.

Morgan Parry (8)
Pen-Y-Fai CW Primary School

The Life Of The Iron Man

The Iron Man was dark and misty like the fog
He was as tall as a gigantic house
He stood in the spooky night
It was a frightening sight
His iron body was as strong as a brick
And his leg could do a mighty kick
But this was only some of his little tricks.

Cameron Breheny (8)
Pen-Y-Fai CW Primary School

That Day

There in a tree
Two headlamp eyes were watching
The *Iron Man!*
As dark as a castle,
He purred as timid as a kitten,
Fast, as quick as lightning,
But no, the Iron Man blew fire,
And Hogarth was a liar.

Lauren Sheppard (8)
Pen-Y-Fai CW Primary School

The Iron Man

There he was walking and bumped into Hogarth
The Iron Man was as strong as a shining black brick wall
And as long as a silver hall
Hogarth was as small as a squeaking coloured mouse
But the Iron Man was as hard as a stormy, sparkly house
Were they friends or not?

Nia Elizabeth Gregory (7)
Pen-Y-Fai CW Primary School

The Iron Man And His Doing

This giant taller than a house, as rusty as an old car.
The sea below was as blue as the sky above.
His green, headlamp eyes as blinding as the sun.
He found something as big as his thumb, it was a bun.
Quick as a flash he ate it and walked on.
The sun came out with its gleaming shine.
As the Iron Man disappeared into the sea.

Rhiannon McColgan (7)
Pen-Y-Fai CW Primary School

Iron Man By The Sea

The people came out to see
The Iron Man by the sea
He was as friendly as a kitten
Hogarth was as cold as morning ice
As tall as a tower house
As strong as a snorting ox
With a magnetic body he attracted metallic things.

Holly Picton (8)
Pen-Y-Fai CW Primary School

The Iron Man

The Iron Man stood at the top of the rocky cliff
There he stood towering above the bubbling sea
The Iron Man was falling as fast as hailstones
He was as strong as an ox
His body was as shiny as a polished car
He was as tall as a black tower
He continued to fall, that was the last of the *Iron Man!*

Marco Jones (7)
Pen-Y-Fai CW Primary School

Life Of The Iron Man

The people came to see
Two green headlights in a tree
They were as bright as shining silver
His body like a black figure
He was as strong as a vicious ox
As hard as freezing Pluto
And difficult to find, hiding from the crowd.

Nia Parry (8)
Pen-Y-Fai CW Primary School

The Iron Man Biting The Tractor

The Iron Man trudged across the yard
Through the windy, misty rain
His eyes crept as gloomy as the night sky
Heading towards a muddy tractor, as dirty as a filthy fly
Sharp teeth marks as hard as a jagged rock
People running as fast as an electric shock
Shouting at the Iron Man, 'Leave our tractors alone!'

Katie Bellis (8)
Pen-Y-Fai CW Primary School

He's Back, He's Back

All the people come out to see the rusty head in the tree.
The head belongs to the Iron Man
He's tall, black and hard to trap.
The objects reflect on his shiny black body.
Like a star in the sky and a reflection in a mirror.
He's hard to catch, he's large to match.
He's tall, strong, made of metal.
He looks like a new shiny car.
He's as strong as an ox, he's got a friend who's a fox.
'We'll get him, we'll get him sooner or later,' cry the mob.

Emma Sue Davies (8)
Pen-Y-Fai CW Primary School

The Munch Crunch Of The Iron Man

The Iron Man ran to the metal fan
He was as strong as a rock
He was as gloomy as night
He was as hard as ice.

George Morgan (8)
Pen-Y-Fai CW Primary School

The Iron Man's Revenge

The people so shocked to see
the Iron Man's head in a tree.
The lights were as bright as the blazing sun
and they blinded everyone.
He was as hard as solid steel
and as fat as a monster truck wheel.
The Iron Man had come back for revenge!

Sebastian Waters-Hussain (8)
Pen-Y-Fai CW Primary School

The Iron Man's Big Revenge

A strange-looking figure came down the hill,
With a battered black wheel in his mouth.
As quiet as a mouse he chewed all the tractor up.
He was as light as a feather, but as big as a bull.
As hard as a rock, he smashed the broken cars.
The Iron Man was as strong as a ferocious lion
But the Iron Man was later, never seen.

Lauren Bigley (8)
Pen-Y-Fai CW Primary School

Is It Him?

There appears the two lights in a bush
Then I see the two metal legs
Can it be as I see?
The sea says, *'Hush,* yes, it's me.'
It must mean the Iron Man is near
The beach is loud and clear
His giant black claw as mighty as the waves
The Iron Man crushes his way through the junk.

Alys Davies (8)
Pen-Y-Fai CW Primary School

Squash Time

The Iron Man was in a tree
And everyone came out to see
He was as strong as a mighty ox
And found a chunky old box
I saw the Iron Man as fast as a bee
He was as strong as dark black coffee
And he stuck everyone together
And he mashed their soft heads together.

Jack McEachen (7)
Pen-Y-Fai CW Primary School

Saint Melangell

S ix hunters went to Llangynog
A nd their dogs and horses too
I n the meantime a hare caught their eye
N ext, they chased the hare, it stopped
T here was a beautiful princess from Ireland before them.

M elangell was her name
E ver so gently the hare hid under her dress
L ooking so pretty in her fine clothes
A ll she wanted was a church and a convent
N ext the land was hers
G od answered all her prayers
E very single one of them
L ater she became 'patron saint of hares'
L ife went on well as a patron saint.

Kathryn Hof (9)
Pen-Y-Fai CW Primary School

Saint Melangell

S ome suspicious huntsmen went to Llangynog
A nd glanced at a hare
I mmediately they began to chase
N ext the hare had disappeared
T o under

M elangell's long dress
E ventually she said her prayer
'L et live the little hare'
A church and a convent was her wish
N ow he said, 'I will
G ive you a church and a convent'
E ventually she finished her prayer and the
L ittle hare escaped
L langynog was the special place to save that hare.

Rosie Upton (8)
Pen-Y-Fai CW Primary School

Saint Melangell

S aint Melangell
A hare was running from hunters
I n Llangynog
N ever knowing
T hat they would meet

M elangell
E ven the hare was there
L ater the dogs
A nd the horses stopped.
N ext one of the men
G ot his lips stuck
E ven Brochwel stopped chasing hares.
L et there be no chasing hares in
L langynog.

Jac David (9)
Pen-Y-Fai CW Primary School

Saint Melangell

S uper hunters came to the country at Llangynog
A t their surprise they saw a hare running along
I mmediately they chased after the hare
N ext to their surprise, the dogs stopped
T he hunters ordered the dogs to carry on.

'M ove along,' shouted the leader called Brochwel
E very horse stopped after a few minutes
'L ovely, the horses have stopped now'
A fterwards, they saw a woman and the hare was under her dress
'N ever have I seen such a thing,'
'G ood lord how are you?'
E ven though he didn't say it in a very nice voice.
'L ord, my name is Melangell, I want to build a church,
                                        I have no land'
'L et me build a church for you, it will be beautiful.'

Samantha Keagle (9)
Pen-Y-Fai CW Primary School

Saint Melangell

S ome hunters and Brochwel went hunting
A way to the countryside
I n the 8th century
N earby there was a fast hare
T rying to run away from the hunters

M elangell was in a clearing
E very hunter was scared stiff
'L et the hare go,' said Brochwel
A t the sight of the hare running to Melangell
'N o, don't be frightened, I am Melangell, an Irish princess
G od is my only friend'
E ventually Brochwel said to the hunters, 'Stop!'
L ady Melangell wanted to build a church
L egends are like fake stories.

Jonathan Westrop (9)
Pen-Y-Fai CW Primary School

Saint Melangell

S ome hunters chased a hare.
A pack of dogs in front.
I can hear the horses' hooves.
N ervous hare running for his life.
T he hunters tracking the hare down.

M elangell protected the hare.
E very dog was on the chase.
L eaving the hunters, the dogs stood still
A fraid of something.
N ervous to even move.
G etting ready to strike.
E very horse stopped.
L eaving the hunters.
L ady Melangell said, 'Will you build a church for me?'
    And one of the horsemen said, 'Yes.'

Alexander Kemble (8)
Pen-Y-Fai CW Primary School

Saint Melangell

S ome suspicious hunters were in the country
A group of them were hunting a hare
I n a wood they chased him and lost sight of him and carried on
N ow they reached the clearing of the wood
T here was a girl praying to God with the hare in her dress

M elangell got up and protected the hare from them
E ver so softly Brochwel whispered, 'Why aren't the
    animals moving?
'L ady move away.'
    'No!' she said. A hunter blew his horn, his wet lips got stuck
A ll of them laughed. She said, 'I've been here for 15 years,
    I ran away from my groom to be.
N asty man he was, I've always wanted my own land
    I've no money.'
'G reen land?' said Brochwel, 'yes, you have some of mine.
    'Thanks.
E ventually I will have a church and a convent'
L ovely Melangell became patron saint of hares.
L ife was safe for the hares and Saint Melangell.

Ellen Devereux (9)
Pen-Y-Fai CW Primary School

Ode To Hand Cream

O' hand cream,
I treasure your click-on lid
I hail your smooth white body,
My hands tremble when I squeeze out your silky cream
I adore it being rubbed deep into my hands,
I will never use another cream except you,
You are my joy, my passion -
My life.

Ben Green (10)
Pen-Y-Fai CW Primary School

Oh To Be A Swimmer

Chorus
Butterfly, backstroke, breaststroke, front crawl.
Butterfly, backstroke, breaststroke, front crawl.

The training is hard, the water is cold,
I have to keep on going to win that gold.

Butterfly, backstroke, breaststroke, front crawl.
Butterfly, backstroke, breaststroke, front crawl.

The training intense, the gala draws near,
My tumble-turns are better, but there's water in my ear!

Butterfly, backstroke, breaststroke, front crawl.
Butterfly, backstroke, breaststroke, front crawl.

Towel, trunks, hat and goggles, my bag is now packed,
The bus is almost leaving and I'm already whacked!

Butterfly, backstroke, breaststroke, front crawl.
Butterfly, backstroke, breaststroke, front crawl.

The noise around the pool is massive, the crowd is already cheering.
Our coach is calling my race now and I can hardly hear him.

Butterfly, backstroke, breaststroke, front crawl.
Butterfly, backstroke, breaststroke, front crawl.

The time for nerves is over now, I'm moving to the block,
I'm focused and I'm ready, as steady as a rock.

Butterfly, backstroke, breaststroke, front crawl.
Butterfly, backstroke, breaststroke, front crawl.

'Take your marks' the whistle blows, I'm reaching for my dive,
The time is right, the race is on and now I feel alive.

Butterfly, backstroke, breaststroke, front crawl.
Butterfly, backstroke, breaststroke, front crawl.

Streamlined through the water fast, 25 metres done,
The competition's heating up, I'll sprint, I've touched, *I've won!*

Butterfly, backstroke, breaststroke, front crawl.
Butterfly, backstroke, breaststroke, front crawl.

My time, I can't believe it! I've beaten my personal best,
I'll take my place, collect my prize, a gold medal to put with the rest!

Butterfly, backstroke, breaststroke, front crawl.
Butterfly, backstroke, breaststroke, front crawl.

I've shaken hands with all the lads, they really are good sports.
We're back on the bus, ready to leave, oh heck,
                                    I've forgotten my shorts.

Butterfly, backstroke, breaststroke, front crawl.
Butterfly, backstroke, breaststroke, front crawl.

Back in training, improving still, I sometimes dare to think,
If I can represent my country, that medal might soon be Olympic!

Butterfly, backstroke, breaststroke, front crawl.
It doesn't matter which stroke, I can do them all!

Mark Byron Ennis (10)
Pen-Y-Fai CW Primary School

Ode To A Pencil Case

Oh wonderful pencil case,
I love and admire your blackness.
It is a beauty to my eyes.
I hail your smooth-like body.
The symbols on you represent the style within you.
Without you my life is incomplete.
My pens will play havoc rolling around everywhere.
I need you perched by my side to keep me company.
I envy you for what you can do.
I wish I could hold pens like you.
Without you pencils would overrule the world.
But you will conquer them.
I will never look at another perky pencil case again.
You are glorious, oh pencil case.
You are my pencil case!

Jack Davies (11)
Pen-Y-Fai CW Primary School

Memory Card

Oh, memory card, so wondrous, perfect and smooth.
I appreciate the black colour and blue patch,
Which fills my eye with happiness.
You never forget saved games.
I admire your technology filled with 8.895KB.
You are the saviour of games.
When I touch you, you make me tremble with joy.
You are the life-giver to games.
Without you my games and console are useless to me.
You are the master of copiers.
You are the real joy-giver and the apple of my console.
Never shall I discard you.
I adore the way you slip inside the computer.
You are not just any memory,
You are my memory card!

Yacoob Rossaye (11)
Pen-Y-Fai CW Primary School

Saint Melangell

S ome hunters went to Llangynog
A nd glanced at a hare
I mmediately they started to race
N ext the hare went sprinting
T hey were shocked that the hare had gone

M elangell came out
E ven though she was a girl, she adored the hare
L ively, she jumped to protect the hare
A nd the hunters were scared
'N ow,' she said, 'I'd like to make a church.
G od would want me to do that.'
E ventually she told her sad story
L uckily the hare had escaped
L langynog was the saviour for the hare.

Holly Hopkins (9)
Pen-Y-Fai CW Primary School

Death Wish

My last moments are given to you hoping that you will cherish
And respect me the way I do you.

To my amazing sister,
I offer to you my smile,
So that you stay strong and keep smiling.

To my beloved mum,
I bestow my mind filled with memories of all the good times we had,
So that you remember and keep them in your heart.

To my dearest dad,
I leave you my bravery,
So you stand up for yourself and never give in, just follow your heart.

To Heidi, my lovely cat,
I leave you my courage,
So you can play on and live a happy life without me.

To my friends,
I donate you luck and forever friendship,
So we can still be friends even if I'm not by your side.

To you all, my adorable family,
I give you my heart, soul and everlasting love,
So that you remember me as I am now, not as I leave you.

Now it is time for me to leave you to go and rest in peace,
I may not see you ever again but at least I had the chance.
So now it is time for me to say goodbye for now my time is up.

Abigail Trigg (10)
Pen-Y-Fai CW Primary School

A Man Called Joseph . . .

A man called Joseph one day
Built a house of clay
He filled it with spice
Which wasn't very nice
Then the wind came and blew it away!

Scott Downie (10)
Pen-Y-Fai CW Primary School

Fireworks

Rockets:

Rockets, rockets, everywhere,
Make you look, stop and stare,
If you see one that flares,
Make it known that you were there.

Catherine Wheel:

Catherine wheel, hear it squeal,
Make it really reel and reel,
If the wheel stops its squeal,
Light another, then
Make it cycle again.

Fountains:

Here's a fountain, isn't it pretty?
Sparkling high above the city,
Shines so bright,
You don't need a light,
And a good time was had by all tonight.

Scott Walton (10)
Pen-Y-Fai CW Primary School

What Is The Sun?

It is a ball of molten lava
Shooting through the sky.

It is a yellow tennis ball
Flying over the net of a tennis court.

It is a fiery comet
Colliding with a shooting star.

It is a spherical piece of gold
Just sitting there in a bank.

Adam Leppard (10)
Pen-Y-Fai CW Primary School

My Last Ten Minutes

My last ten minutes are spared for you,
My beloved wife I offer a hundred red roses
And my broken heart forever more.
And to my three little girls, I ask you to keep your spirits high
Because Daddy will always be there for you.
To the last member of my wonderful family,
My only son, I pass on love and an endless memory of us playing
So he can remember the good times we shared together.
And to my country, Wales, I donate my courage,
So that you will always have my spirit to fight.
To my enemy
I hope you rot in Hell.
They could not take my life without me first remembering
My wife and children.
I am not dead, I am in your hearts and I will never leave your side -
I promise!

Adam Lee Griffin (11)
Pen-Y-Fai CW Primary School

The Moon

What is the moon?

Is it ice
Or maybe it's cheese with mice?

It could be a boat boating,
Or even a balloon floating.

It may be a big, white ball,
Or a head of someone tall.

I do not know what it is.

What do you think?

Bethan Pascoe (11)
Pen-Y-Fai CW Primary School

Death

Death is fatal, you cannot survive,
However much you work and strive.
It's impossible to fool death,
It always seems to catch your breath.
Your heart stops thudding, there's shooting pains,
Your blood stops pumping through your veins.
You fall down hard with a mighty thud,
Then you're buried in the mud.
Next you go to Heaven or Hell,
This depends if you behaved well.
So always try your best,
Because life is your test.

Eleri Pritchard (10)
Pen-Y-Fai CW Primary School

My Last Ten Minutes

My last ten minutes
I give to you
Remember me like I'll remember you,
To my beloved wife, I can't give you anything
But my heart and my soul,
To my adventurous son, I offer you my courage
So that you can lead our family to victory and good deeds,
And to my enemy, I leave you hatred and the
Devil's unknown curse to haunt you forever.

To my family, my last ten minutes were given to you,
I love you more than I ever have before.

Morgan Owen (11)
Pen-Y-Fai CW Primary School

Spider, Spider

Spider, spider, big and black
Scary creature running fast
Big long legs from its back
Runs out the door, gone at last

Now I'm frightened, he comes again
Hairy legs moving quick
Getting closer as fast as a plane
I've got to move, be very slick

Jump over him as he runs
Now I'm ahead I get to the door
Open quickly, here he comes
Passes by me across the floor

Slam!

Jasmine Gill (10)
Pen-Y-Fai CW Primary School

Friendship!

Friendship is a knot you
Can never untie,
A friend is a person you
Can always rely,
If that knot ever comes
Apart,
Then that friend is not
A real friend that would warm
Your heart.

Kelly Oakley (11)
Pen-Y-Fai CW Primary School

Listen

Rustle! Rustle!
There he goes again
Breaking up his bed.
My naughty rabbit.

Rustle! Rustle!
Ripping all the paper
Dragging it down the tunnel,
You can hear him scratching,
Scuffling,
Sniffling,
Twitching.

There he goes again,
My naughty
Rabbit.

Emily Whittle (9)
St John's School, Porthcawl

Listen

Bang! Bang!
More guns firing
Getting closer
Closer
And closer.

Here I am
Lying in my burrow
My heart thumping
For hours on end.

Are they getting closer?
Yes!

Dylan Hopkins (8)
St John's School, Porthcawl

Listen

Listen to my mum calling,
Listen to my sister crunching,
Listen to the phone ringing,
Listen to the door barking,
Listen to the doorbell ringing,
Listen to the TV booming,
Listen to the man on the TV.

Listen to the lawnmower cutting,
Listen to the traffic moving,
Listen to the neighbours talking,
Listen to the postman calling,
Listen to the playing children,
Listen to the builders building,
Listen to the birds flying,
Listen to my mum calling.

Tom Brown (8)
St John's School, Porthcawl

Listen

During the night I listen to things,
Things that have legs
And things that have wings.
There was one little bird and then another,
And then quietly came in my mother.
'It's nearly here,
It's nearly here,' she said.
I was wondering what it was.
I looked out of the window,
I saw birds flying - each one a different way
Yes, of course. That thing was . . .
                         Day!

Ross Murray (8)
St John's School, Porthcawl

Listen

Listen to the door
slam!
Listen to the seatbelt
click!
Listen to the engine
rev!
Listen to the car
speed!
How smooth it can be.

Listen to the horn
beep!
Listen to the indicators
tick-tock!
Listen to the brakes
screech!
Listen to the windscreen wipers
back and forth
back and forth
What a noisy car!

Henry Thomas Smout (9)
St John's School, Porthcawl

Space

Space is vast
Space is dark
Space has wondrous planets
Space has sparkling stars.

I'm travelling to Mars
I'm racing to the moon
Through the dark night sky
Through the zooming comets.

You can speed to space in a rocket
You can drive to space in a car
But I don't think you'd get very far.

Alice Williams (11)
St John's School, Porthcawl

The Sea

The sea is blue
The fish are swimming in shoals
There is a shipwreck under the seabed
Jewels, silver and gold are there.

Waves are rolling over the wreck
Bottles are crashing on the sand
With messages or a map inside
Empty containers floating by.

A little map showing a treasure chest
A little draught of wind and the map is gone
An old book floating by
A box buried in the sand clutching its treasure.

Shellfish on the sand
Crabs are scuttling by
Shrimps are swimming in the rock pools
An octopus parachutes to the bottom of the sea.

Samantha Richardson (9)
St John's School, Porthcawl

Listen

'Listen!'
I'm in a haunted house
All alone,
Listen to the thunder crashing,
Listen to the spiders crawling,
Listen to the ghosts moaning,
Listen to the skeletons rattling,
Listen to the werewolves howling,
Listen to the bats flapping,
Listen to the owls hooting,
Listen to Mum and Dad shouting,
Phew!
It was all just a dream.

Michael Raymond (9)
St John's School, Porthcawl

Listen

I'm in a mansion,
It's full of noises,
It looks haunted,
What's that?
There's something scattering.

'Argh.'
Listen,
I think it's thunder.

A ghost!
Listen, it's only the wind
Climbing the creaking stairs.

What's that?
Listen,
It's only the stairs.

Spiders!
Listen,
It's only the rain.

Ghosts playing drums!
Listen,
It's only the clock,
After all that, I should have listened more carefully.

Joe Strong (9)
St John's School, Porthcawl

Listen

Listen to the wind blowing the trees side by side
Listen to the storm crashing and banging
Listen to the children playing games
Listen to the TV blaring all night.
Here I am lying in bed listening to the things
That must be said.

Callum Hawker (8)
St John's School, Porthcawl

Space

Space is like a gigantic bowl,
Full of thick, thick black soup.
There are nine vegetables in this soup,
All different shapes and sizes.

Mercury is munchable
Venus is very tasty
Earth is edible
Mars is marshmallowy
Jupiter is just right
Saturn is scrumptious
Uranus is unbelievable
Neptune is nutritious
Pluto is perfect

And the sun, the sun is so, so
                            spicy!

Verity Smout (11)
St John's School, Porthcawl

Listen

Listen to the animals
Listen to the cat miaowing
Listen to the dog barking
Listen to the pig honking
Listen to the people talking
Listen to the TV booming
Listen to the babies crying
Listen to the adults laughing
Listen to the clock ticking
Listen to the thunder roaring
Listen to the lightning crashing
Listen to the rain splattering and thumping
Listen to my mum calling me in for tea.

Elliot Jones (8)
St John's School, Porthcawl

Listen

I'm in a haunted mansion
Full of noises
Listen!
What's that?
Creak!
Downstairs I went
Downstairs I crept
Listen!
'Arooo!'
The howling of a werewolf
Listen!
'Whooo!'
The groan of a ghost.

Listen!
Clackity clackity
Skeleton bones
Listen!
Rustle
The scuttling of a spider,
Rustle, rustle!

Daniel Shearer (9)
St John's School, Porthcawl

Listen

Listen to the trees crunching
Listen to the wind whistling
Listen to my window crashing
Listen to the angry thunder
Listen to the flashing lightning
Kaboom!

Here I am
Snuggling in my bed
Safe and sound
Just listening.

Francesca Groom (9)
St John's School, Porthcawl

Space

I'm trapped,
Not enough space,
Not enough space to move - to think - to breathe
I'm trapped. My head is spinning.

How I long to be free,
To think - to move - to breathe
I long for space,
To feel the air in my face

But suddenly!

I feel a breath of a breeze
The bars that have kept me imprisoned
Have all gone,
Finally I am free!

Isaac Lake (11)
St John's School, Porthcawl

Listen

Listen to the sound of a raindrop
Rushing down my bedroom window,
Pitter-patter, pitter-patter.

Listen to the trees creaking,
In the savage wind,
Pitter-patter, pitter-patter.

Thunder crashing,
Lightning storming down,
Pitter-patter, pitter-patter.

But I'm safe,
I'm fine,
I'm just listening.

Elan Edry (8)
St John's School, Porthcawl

The Sea

I went swimming this morning,
Searching for rare fish
I had no idea what I would find.

I dived into the sea
Swam deeper, deeper towards the seabed.
Instead I found a shipwreck.
I swam through the porthole
There were all types of fish
To my delight I saw a stingray.

I quickly moved from room to room
Trying to find more fish,
Wait a minute! What is this?
A treasure trove!
Silver and gold coins,
Diamonds and a golden ring.

I spied a shark,
Quickly I grabbed the treasure
Swam frantically to the shore
Never to go back again!

George Mead (9)
St John's School, Porthcawl

Outer Space

O uter space is a dark place
U nder a canopy of planets and stars
T he planets are bare like lost cities
E verywhere you look is darkness
R ound the planets silently spin.

S pace is confusing
P lanets plummet through a bottomless pit
A nywhere you go, the endless flow of darkness is there
C reeping into every cave and crater
E ndless space. Too much space!

Callum Williamson (10)
St John's School, Porthcawl

The Sea

Amazing as the sea
Can be
It is so mysterious

Stripes of red and white
From protected lionfish
A squid
Ready for dinner

Conger eels
Hide in wreck
Stingrays hide
Under the sand

Sea turtles crawl along the beach
Where predators can't reach

Sardines are in a shoal
Hammerhead sharks
The seabed patrol

The seabed is so pretty
With coral of all colours
Many more mysteries
To be discovered.

Ieuan Briers (10)
St John's School, Porthcawl

Listen

Listen to my poem
Listen all day long
Listen for just a second
You can listen if you want
Listen, just listen
All night long.

My poem is not perfect,
My poem is not long,
Pretty please, can you listen to my poem?

Theo Clarke (9)
St John's School, Porthcawl

The Sea

Today I went out on my fishing boat,
I took my fishing rod and wetsuit
It was a lovely morning, the sun was shining
Everyone was at the beach
Even people I had not seen before.

The sea was clear as glass
Looking for some spectacular fish,
Further and further out to sea
Going deeper into the deep blue ocean.

I eventually found what I was looking for
Some squid, octopus and a jellyfish
I tried to catch one with my net
But they swam away out of sight.

It took me a while to get my catch
Only the tasty ones though
Then it started to pour down with rain
I tried to find shelter
Land was ahead.

Further and further I had to climb
Upon a rock so steep
And waited till the break of dawn
To be rescued safe and sound.

Aaron James (9)
St John's School, Porthcawl

Space

Space! I need space,
No room to play,
No room to move,
No room to think!
Loud, noisy,
Smells of cigarettes,
Where am I?

Space, lots of it!
What shall I do?
What shall I say?
What shall I look at?
Quiet and peaceful
Where am I?

Space, my space!
To do what I want,
To say what I feel,
No one to bother me,
No one to tell me what to do.
My world!
My
Space!

Joe Clarke (10)
St John's School, Porthcawl

The Sea

The sea is big and blue
The waves keep splashing along the shore
The fish swim all day long
The people play in the sea.

The sea holds lots of creatures
Most of them are harmless
Some of them are dangerous
My favourite creature is the blue whale.

There's lots of things to collect
Like shells and pebbles
Pieces of string, dried seaweed
Driftwood and cuttlefish.

People paddle in the rock pools
To wash off the sand
It is warmer than the sea
Watch out for the crabs!

The sea is very beautiful
But the waves sometimes drag you down
Deep into the bottomless pit
No turning back.

Dylan Griffiths (10)
St John's School, Porthcawl

The Sea

T he place we love to come is the sea
H ope for a nice day to enjoy the beach
E veryone comes for an hour of fun.

S ea and sun, they make for a fun play
E very day the fun and games take place
A nd we spend such time with family and friends.

Bradley John (11)
St John's School, Porthcawl

The Sea

I went on a fishing trip,
To the ocean waves,
Oh, I thought, *I've caught something big,*
As my rod was pulling away.

I wound, wound, my fishing rod,
Until I saw an . . . octopus tentacle,
I rowed, rowed, and rowed some more,
The octopus still pulled me into the sea.

I saw the billowing waves,
Fish of all kinds swimming happily,
The water changed to a deeper shade of blue,
I saw him open his mouth and . . .

His tentacles were pulling me closer,
Towards his ugly mouth,
Yuck! It was disgusting,
I was desperate to escape.

I had a torch, quickly flashed it in his eyes,
I frantically swam back to surface,
Up went the flare,
I was yanked to rescue by air.

James Kearle (9)
St John's School, Porthcawl

What Is Blue?

Blue is the sea splashing all about.
Blue is a blueberry, squish, squish.
A dolphin is blue jumping about.
A shark is blue, crunch, crunch.
Blue is the colour of hair gel.
Can you imagine living without it?

Joshua Faitas (8)
St Mary's Catholic Primary School, Bridgend

Space

Silver stars floating in the burning sky
Rocks moving and spinning
Men are in the rockets
Burning world moving
The darkness of the moon
Birds sing. Falling faster
Dull darkness of the moon
Dull darkness
The blackness of space.

Roisín Ellis (8)
St Mary's Catholic Primary School, Bridgend

In Space

I am the silver bird
Falling in the darkness of the moon.
The rockets are empty
And I sing in the day.
The rocks are floating
And the stars are glowing.

William Austin (8)
St Mary's Catholic Primary School, Bridgend

In Space

In the sky
the moon burns
and turns in the darkness.
Spacemen travel
above rocks and stars.
Lightning clings
in the blackness.

Bethany Louise Hammond (7)
St Mary's Catholic Primary School, Bridgend

Fireworks

In the sky Catherine wheels
whirling above Earth.
Each one white and blue
and orange.
Showers fall like petals.
Wonderful rockets rise.
Magic unfolds sudden bursts.
Miracles like buds.

Jordan Ryan (8)
St Mary's Catholic Primary School, Bridgend

Dragon

Look out for the mysterious maroon dragon!
His eyes are as bright as the sunbeams.
His teeth are as sharp as a spiky coffin.
His breath is as hot as a chilli
And he's as frightening as Queen Elizabeth I.
Look out for the mysterious maroon dragon.

Catherine Gardiner (9)
St Mary's Catholic Primary School, Bridgend

Fireworks

F ireworks are beautiful.
I love Catherine wheels.
R ockets and Catherine wheels.
E van loves sparklers.
W e love fireworks.
O ne has sparklers.
R ockets are the best.
K ids love fireworks.
S parklers are great!

Evan Lister (8)
St Mary's Catholic Primary School, Bridgend

The Lonely Dump Haikus

The fire in the pit
All the flames already lit
Orange, yellow, red.

Grassy is the dump
Messy children all around
Fossils, bottles too.

Slime up the green wall
All the leftover wrappers
A stony, big cave.

Cats are there as well
The dump is so dangerous
Don't go over there.

Grass is all soggy
The tyres are all broken
It is the big dump!

Zoe-Marie Harrison (9)
St Mary's Catholic Primary School, Bridgend

Fireworks

In the night sky
Upon the Earth
Wonderful Catherine wheels
Burst and shake
Rockets whirling orange
and blue
Suddenly magic marigolds
rise and fall.
Candles begin to make petals.

James Stephens (7)
St Mary's Catholic Primary School, Bridgend

Why?

War is filled with horror
War is filled with death
When bombs drop down they're as deadly as a demon
As destructive as death
Innocent people dying
Innocent people crying
Why should people die?
Why should people cry?
When torpedoes fire black smoke rises
It's as black as the inside of a cave
War is sad
War is bad
When you sleep at dawn
You might not taste the morn
Why should people suffer? Why? Why?
Why should people die? Why? Why?
Why should people cry? Why? Why?

Gervaise Turbervill (10)
St Mary's Catholic Primary School, Bridgend

Fireworks

In the night
Catherine wheels
make magic upon
the blue sky, and
flowers unfold in
wonderful orange
showers falling
to earth
fiery petals melt and
shake like trees.

Emily Read (8)
St Mary's Catholic Primary School, Bridgend

What Is Yellow?

Yellow is the sun shining on the sea.
Yellow is the colour that makes me happy.
Yellow is when movies make me sad.
Yellow is the computer screen.

Jessica Williams (8)
St Mary's Catholic Primary School, Bridgend

What Is Pink?

Pink is a pig
On the farm.
Pink is a party dress
In the disco.
Pink is candyfloss
On a stick.
Pink is paper
For a letter for my friend.
Roses are pink
Smelling so sweet.
Pink is pretty
I like pink.

Laurie Williams (8)
St Mary's Catholic Primary School, Bridgend

What Is Green?

Green is a frog
Jumpy and squidgy.
Green is scary
Like an alien.
Green monsters scare the aliens.
Grasshoppers live in greenhouses
I like green.

Zachary Whelan (7)
St Mary's Catholic Primary School, Bridgend

Fireworks

Blue flames burst upon the sky
Rockets and Catherine wheels.
Miraculous Roman candles unfold -
Crimson and orange.
Magic buds falling in showers
From the sky.

Liam Phillips (8)
St Mary's Catholic Primary School, Bridgend

The Dump Haikus

Dirty, smelly dump
The rubbish flew everywhere
It is disgusting

Dangerous and high
Tins rattle in the dark dump
Rusty and smelly.

Sam Burke (9)
St Mary's Catholic Primary School, Bridgend

What Is Yellow?

Yellow is the sun that shines in the sky.
Buttercups are yellow, shiny and bright.
The middle of a daisy is yellow too.
Yellow makes me happy
And warm inside.
I like yellow.

Daniel Burke (8)
St Mary's Catholic Primary School, Bridgend

Boredom

Boredom is sitting quietly for the slow teacher to arrive.
Boredom is working on your atrocious handwriting.
Boredom is staying in and finishing off your dull work during break
Boredom is playing with the dull, uninteresting wet play games.
Boredom is a gloomy Frusli bar for break - again.
Boredom is a dull dissatisfying Greek myth.
Boredom is walking gloomily to your dismal house.
Boredom is a horrible way of life.

Sam Evans (10)
St Mary's Catholic Primary School, Bridgend

What Is Blue?

Blue is the sea splashing about.
Blue is the colour of a big, fat, poisonous frog.
Blue is the colour of a crawling lizard.
Blue is a dolphin jumping in the sea.
Blue is the colour of a dangerous shark.
Blue is the colour of the sky high above.
Blue reminds me of blueberries.

Kate Pearson (7)
St Mary's Catholic Primary School, Bridgend

Happiness

Happiness is going horse riding with my sister
Happiness is walking to go and see my horse
Happiness is hearing him whining as he sees me
Happiness is grooming my horse with it swishing its tail
Happiness is riding my horse on the green, swishing grass
Happiness is feeding my horse and giving it splashing water
Happiness is caring for my horse and loving him
Happiness is him rubbing his neck against me
Happiness is walking home after a gallop with the wind in my hair.

Jessica Ellis (9)
St Mary's Catholic Primary School, Bridgend

Waterfall

At last I have found the waterfall,
Rushing sounds everywhere,
Like a white horse jumping down, down.

I wait, determined to see what's next,
It's peaceful and quiet,
It's late in time.

It's so amazing when I'm gazing,
Drip-drop, splish, splosh, splash.

I put my hand through the water
That's rushing out onto the sand,
It's winking, it's sinking,
I wonder what it's thinking?

I don't know what to do or say,
On this morning on this day.

Hannah Vivian-Byrne (10)
St Mary's Catholic Primary School, Bridgend

What Is White?

White is a cloud
Moving and sparkling.
White is feeling ill.
White is snow like a snowman,
Sometimes white is really cold ice.
White sticks to your hand.
White is the petal of a daisy.
White is the toilet factory.
I write on white paper,
I rub out with a white rubber.
My favourite colour is white.

Paige-Charlotte Harrison (9)
St Mary's Catholic Primary School, Bridgend

The Hopeless Dump Haikus

Trees are tumbling down
At the rainy rainforest
And at the chalk pit.

A white and deep pit
Bottles, cans, shattered around
Fossils never found.

Cars and bikes destroyed
Never ridden anymore
In the stinky dump.

Tins and cans scattered
Broken glass shattered fiercely
White and muddy pit.

Gabriel Trio (8)
St Mary's Catholic Primary School, Bridgend

The Dump

The dump is muddy
rusty, dusty and smoky
tins, bins, stones, bones, dim.

It's messy and cold
dark and damp, rotten and black
slimy and dirty.

Bottles everywhere
dirty carpets, bent and grey
shabby and smelly.

Metal brass bed knobs.
who wants to go there? Not me!
Black and dangerous

Caroline Riley (9)
St Mary's Catholic Primary School, Bridgend

The Wasted Countryside Tankas

Fossils and bottles!
Deserted, spooky, scary!
Rotten apples stink!
It is layered with rubbish!
Nobody likes the new dump!

It is breathtaking!
It is dark, lonely, creepy!
Ivy is growing!
There's bits of food everywhere!
Wish the countryside was back!

Skins and tins and stones!
Trees are falling to the ground!
Disgusting rubbish!
Rotten apples and rank food!
People say it's dangerous!

Louise Doran (9)
St Mary's Catholic Primary School, Bridgend

The Dumping Ground - Haikus

Ivy on the side
'Keep out' signs around the side
Bikes in the middle.

The dump is messy
The moon is in the dark sky
That cannot be seen.

Bikes are on the floor
And rubbish on the dark floor
This is an old dump.

Thomas Enos (8)
St Mary's Catholic Primary School, Bridgend

No Chance For The Dump Tankas

No one remembers
What they have done to the dump
South of the river
Fish used to swim there, not now
For the water is dirty

Grass is lined with slime
Once was lovely, now destroyed
Ranks hang everywhere
No plant has a chance to live
No survivors in the dump

Once was blue, now black
Rusty tins and bins, so rank
Smelly, dangerous
Rank brass bed knobs are spiky
Everything is dangerous.

Rónan Vivian-Byrne (8)
St Mary's Catholic Primary School, Bridgend

Dumping Ground Haikus

Skins and tins, brass beds
Old and cold, spooky, spiky
Messy, slimy things

Carpets, old, smelly
Creepy, smelly, up and down
Rubbish everywhere

Black and messy things
Everywhere full of rubbish
Stones and bones, steel wheels.

Aimee Jones (9)
St Mary's Catholic Primary School, Bridgend

Surprise

Surprise is when I open the door and see my family ready to celebrate
my birthday
Surprise is having my favourite meal on my special day
Surprise is my shocked face on seeing my friends coming to celebrate
my birthday
Surprise is being amazed on seeing my presents
Surprise is seeing so many happy faces
Surprise is receiving so many cards
Surprise is going into the kitchen and seeing my candles lit
Surprise is my family singing 'Happy Birthday'
Surprise is eating my delicious cake
Surprise is the joy of life!

Daniel Evans (10)
St Mary's Catholic Primary School, Bridgend

Smelly Dump Haikus

The dump is smelly
A load of old bits and bobs
An old picture frame

Big bikes with flat tyres
Spiders, beetles everywhere
Green grass very tall

A load of old clothes
Trees near lakes nearly falling
Old clothes are too small

It used to be nice
Spiky pieces sticking out
It is unpleasant.

Lucy McPhee (8)
St Mary's Catholic Primary School, Bridgend

A Horrible Dump Tankas

Nothing is here now
What have people done to dumps?
Skins and tins cover
There is metal over there
You had better go away

Dirty and smelly
Slimy stones have fallen down
You would not survive
There is rusty, old paint cans
You would not want to go there

How could you breathe there?
People do not live near it
Wrecked trees hanging down
Horrible mats wrecked badly
You wouldn't want to go there.

Ross Andrew (9)
St Mary's Catholic Primary School, Bridgend

Surprise

A surprise is something that makes you jump
A surprise is a party full of joy
A surprise is getting an extra present
A surprise is tearing off the gleaming paper
A surprise is having an extra play at school
A surprise is aunty coming for a visit
A surprise is having an old friend to stay
A surprise is snow at Christmas
A surprise is being hit by a snowball
A surprise is waking up and finding the snow all gone.

Troy Collins (9)
St Mary's Catholic Primary School, Bridgend

The Quiet Wood

Here's the quiet wood
Where people would go if they could
But the gate is locked with a bolt
It puts people to a halt.

People chuck rubbish over the gate instead of in a bin
Smudged all over their face is a big grin
The great monster comes raving towards the wood
The wood would stop it if it could.

The monster is huge like Mount Everest
But the wood is the cleverest
It cuts down trees and digs up the ground
I hope none of the animals can be found.

There's a person who helps the beast destroy
Is it a man or a boy?
It is kept prisoner in a glass box
To destroy the squirrel, badger or fox.

Hannah Bloomfield (10)
St Mary's Catholic Primary School, Bridgend

Surprise

Surprise is the pile of presents to open.
Surprise is seeing your family arrive.
Surprise is seeing lots of colourful balloons.
Surprise is opening up all your exciting gifts.
Surprise is opening the door to friends' happy faces.
Surprise is getting what you really want - a ring!
Surprise is having a grand birthday cake.
Surprise is family and friends singing to me.
Surprise is playing fun games and winning.
Surprise is *surprise!*

Shauni Summers (10)
St Mary's Catholic Primary School, Bridgend

The Steam Engine

Its pistons move
Like a muscular athlete's body
The water boils into steams
Which makes it as fast as the queen
Its boiler swallows black coal
As if it was a piranha shoal
This industrial wonder does its job
Relieving men from their jobs
Its soot comes thick and black
As if it was a black bat
Its red fire bites
As red as a brake light
It throws soot over its shoulder
As if it was a battling soldier
It's fast as a sprinter
Silent as sheep
This extreme engineering
Was the transport better than feet?

Aled Phillips (11)
St Mary's Catholic Primary School, Bridgend

Boredom

Boredom is a dull walk to the bus stop
Boredom is getting onto the gloomy, dreary bus
Boredom is a weary, grey playtime
Boredom is sitting through a glum history lesson
Boredom is an endless English lesson
Boredom is the drone of the teacher reading a tiresome story
Boredom is the buzz of the bus engine
Boredom is walking home from a dull day at school
Boredom is doing tiresome work
Boredom is boredom!

Archan Bhaumik (9)
St Mary's Catholic Primary School, Bridgend

Wasteland Haikus

Bottles and fossils
It is a really rank place
Slime covers the junk

The dump is so rank
The broken glass everywhere
Covering the junk

Rough, spooky, dusty
Rust and rubber everywhere
Rusty, iron, steel

On the floor tins, bins
Carpets, old, smelly, dirty
Damp, quiet, scary

Messy, black, rusty
Brass bed knobs, broken tree roots
It is a let down.

Sophie Hinchen (9)
St Mary's Catholic Primary School, Bridgend

Red

Red is the rose covered in morning dew.
Red is a heart so full of love.
Red is an apple juicy and sweet.
Red is a warm colour on a cold day.
Red is shiny in the glistening wrapping paper.
Red is anger.
Red is hot around the campfire.
Red is a warning to stay away.
Red is the flame flickering high.
Red is the evening sky at the close of day.

Catherine Mainwaring (9)
St Mary's Catholic Primary School, Bridgend

Cats

It's dark and it's as black as burnt bark
Its prey is coming
Stealthy as mice getting cheese
There, ready to pounce
Their eyes are like gems shining
They dash and clash into each other
They can't see, all they hear is shhh
Now it's getting lighter, the river is calm
The fur of the cats is like pillow cases
And their noses are like pink marshmallows
Their paws are as cold as a freezer
And their faces are as cute as a baby
But viscious as a jaguar.

John Ellis (10)
St Mary's Catholic Primary School, Bridgend

Red

Red is a steaming, wonderful colour.
Red is like a glistening bright red rose.
Red is a tropical sunset colour.
Red is like a burning campfire.
Red is a glossy, cheerful colour that brightens my day.
Red is the colour of anger as your blood boils.
Red is the gleaming, shiny colour of a brand new car.
Red is a jolly colourful colour, like rosy cheeks.
Red is the colour of a heart on Valentine's Day.
Red is beautiful, it makes me feel cosy inside.

Grace Emery (9)
St Mary's Catholic Primary School, Bridgend

Family

Family - mums, dads, girls and boys,
Each giving lots of joy,
Always standing by each other,
Like a pack of wolves.

Family - lots of emotions, rows and love,
Always having fun,
Never feeling glum,
Always best of friends.

Family - sometimes annoying, sometimes kind,
Always attending to each others needs,
Sticking together like beads on a bracelet,
Always trying to be happy.

Matthew Pearson (11)
St Mary's Catholic Primary School, Bridgend

The Sky

The night sky, as dark as a room with no light
Lit by the shine off the moon
As beautiful as the view from the top of a mountain
Where owls overhead take flight.

When you wake up the dazzle of the morning sun
Shining into your eyes
Dazzling you with great delight
And not a cloud in the sky.

Night falls again, the moon rises, the stars start to appear
As twinkling as gems, as shiny as diamonds
From where you're standing it looks near
But you know it's far away, far away in the atmosphere.

Gregory Phillips (10)
St Mary's Catholic Primary School, Bridgend

Animals In The Jungle

When you go into the jungle you'll find,
A mouse, a tiger, maybe a sloth.
You may even see a great big moth,
You won't see a tiger sitting at your door,
You might find a slug but not much more.

If you go by a lake you'll find a turtle,
When you go in a field you might find a mouse,
But you won't find an elephant as big as a house,
So when you go into the jungle you will see no better place.
To see a tiger prowling is the best thing to see,
A busy little bumblebee,
A grumpy old lion,
So be aware, when you go in there,
Please do take care!

Hannah Cocks (11)
St Mary's Catholic Primary School, Bridgend

Family

A family is like a bond of love
As peaceful as a gentle dove
Like an army of friends
That will never part
And will stay in my heart for evermore
We will never give up
On and on for evermore
Never leaving anyone behind
And others are never left alone
And people are never thrown
Out of the family.

Joshua Floyd (10)
St Mary's Catholic Primary School, Bridgend

Wildlife

The waterfall is like a gem twinkling
The blackbirds are flying over
As black as a miner's face
The sun is setting, the first star's appearing.

A cat appears in the moonlight
His eyes glowing
Like a candle in darkness
It's a wonderful sight.

The trees are swaying
Back and forth
In the midsummer breeze
As if they were saying something.

Wildlife is the best
The best thing ever
Here to see and watch forever.

Niall Bowerman (10)
St Mary's Catholic Primary School, Bridgend

Happiness

Happiness is waking up on Monday and it's my birthday
Happiness is when I have a colourful, surprise birthday party
Happiness is a merry and cheerful Christmas
Happiness is a joyful celebration - a wedding, or a baby being born
Happiness is a bright summer's day when there is no school
Happiness is when I am with my friends and family
Happiness is feeling the crackling snow on my boots.

Shay Corconan (10)
St Mary's Catholic Primary School, Bridgend

Happiness

Happiness is a holiday
Happiness is getting ready, packing the suitcases
Happiness is loading the car, filling the tank, setting off
Happiness is arriving, seeing the sea sparkling under the sun
Happiness is unpacking my suitcase, sprinting down to the sea
Happiness is building a sandcastle, putting a flag on top
Happiness is enjoying a game of cricket with my family
Happiness is eating scrumptious hot dogs
Happiness is stretched flat out on my back
Happiness is feeling the warmth of the sun on me.

Adam Boon (10)
St Mary's Catholic Primary School, Bridgend

Red

Red is the colour of eyes when you are angry,
Red is a hot, blazing sun,
Red is the glowing, hot flames of the fire,
Red is the colour of faces when they are steaming with hatred,
Red is the colour of a bright red rose for your valentine,
Red is the colour of a delicious wobbly jelly,
Red is the colour of my mum's lips when she goes out,
Red is the colour of delicious strawberries that we pick in the
                                        summer sun
Red is the colour of noses and fingers in the freezing cold weather
Red is the colour of life.

Lucy Hunt (9)
St Mary's Catholic Primary School, Bridgend

Rivers

Through the winter's night the river goes on
As peaceful as a cat sleeping
Through the town it goes
As quiet as a lion prowling through the grass

Up the hill it goes
Through the silent night
Down the hill it goes
As fast as a car whizzing down a road

Keeps on going and going
Sparkling like gems in a treasure chest
On and on it goes
Through the winter's night.

Ben Hampton (11)
St Mary's Catholic Primary School, Bridgend

Red

Red is the warm, tropical sunsets of holidays
Red is the blazing, hot flames of the fire
Red is the colour of hatred
Red is the quick-tempered colour that turns into a rage
Red is a colour that glows in the gloomy dark
Red is the steamy, hot sun on a long summer's day
Red is a colour of warning, so beware!
Red is the colour of your blood when it boils
Red is the colour of the tips of your fingers and toes on a cold,
frosty day.

Jack Parrish (9)
St Mary's Catholic Primary School, Bridgend

Springtime

Petals turning
Blowing in the wind
Like a soft cloud
As warm as a glowing fire
They sing so loud
As warm as a glowing sun
All different colours
All the colours in the world
The daffodil is so gentle
Swinging so softly
When dark comes
They are forgotten
Like a graveyard
Just swinging
There all alone.

Laurel-Paige Jones (10)
St Mary's Catholic Primary School, Bridgend

Red

Red is the colour of the dancing flames in the cosy fire.
Red is the Christmas colour, bright and glowing.
Red is a cheerful colour with lots of warmth in it.
Red is jolly, happy and is the colour of our hearts.
Red is the colour of a single rose, the colour of love.
Red is the colour of an evening sky.
Red is the colour of us on a freezing cold day.
Red is a hot nose colour, it is running through us.
Red is a grand and royal colour.
Red is in us and all around us.

Meryl Hanmer (9)
St Mary's Catholic Primary School, Bridgend

A Faraway Dream

I open my eyes and it feels like a dream
Everyone eating strawberries and cream
All around me is blue, blue sky
Dolphins swim by and you hear their cry
All around this relaxing land
Is covered in white, white sand
This rippling ocean is as clear as glass slippers
Breakfast always served with fresh, fresh kippers
I lie awake
Thinking what I can take
To make the day last longer
Even though I won't be stronger
The sun is now setting orange, yellow and red
While we are getting ready for bed.

Bianca Whelan (11)
St Mary's Catholic Primary School, Bridgend

River

From the spring the water flows
Through the night sky
It runs down the river like a snake
And comes crashing down
Further down the river a waterfall awaits
Down the waterfall the water goes
Crashing down and down
The water squirming down the river
Nearly at its destiny
Eventually the sea awaits
In the night's sky.

Jacob Curtis (10)
St Mary's Catholic Primary School, Bridgend

Boredom

Boredom is staying in the class at playtime trying to work out
a math's problem.
Boredom is waiting in the dinner line to have a cold pizza
and a tasteless chocolate cake.
Boredom is not being able to play on the field in the cold, bleak winter.
Boredom is doing folk dancing instead of doing PE.
Boredom is going out to play a boring game that you don't really
want to play.
Boredom is waiting in the bus line to find out the bus has broken down.
Boredom is waiting for your favourite TV programme to begin.
Boredom is doing your three page English homework.
Boredom is saying your times table over and over again.
Boredom plays a big part in our lives.

Daniel Sacchi (10)
St Mary's Catholic Primary School, Bridgend

Surprise

Surprise is having a mobile phone for my birthday.
Surprise is going on holiday and we're all on our own.
Surprise is having some sunny weather.
Surprise is double maths, when it's supposed to be art.
Surprise is when it starts to snow, a chance to build a snowman.
Surprise is Mum getting us a McDonald's.
Surprise is the new toy with my Happy Meal.
Surprise is waking up on Monday and there is no school.
Surprise is watching 'I'm A Celebrity . . . Get Me Out Of Here'!
Surprise is just something that happens in my life.

Shannon Davis (9)
St Mary's Catholic Primary School, Bridgend

Surprise

Surprise is having a party that I knew nothing about
Surprise is when you open the door with a room full of
colourful presents
Surprise is when you see all your friends waiting
Surprise is celebrating happily with your friends and family patiently
Surprise is opening all the presents which you never thought
you'd have
Surprise is having the bubbly lemonade and delicious food
Surprise is when cheerful friends make you laugh
Surprise is seeing my family wishing me 'Happy Birthday'
Surprise is all these surprises on your birthday
Surprise is something you didn't know about.

Lauren Sadler (10)
St Mary's Catholic Primary School, Bridgend

Boredom

Boredom is waiting gloomily for the slow bus.
Boredom is sitting, cheerless in class waiting for the teacher to arrive.
Boredom is working out the tedious answers to dismal maths sums.
Boredom is the bleak and uninteresting wet play games.
Boredom is listening to the teacher talk on and on about boring work.
Boredom is finishing fatiguing English work and checking it's correct.
Boredom is singing and listening in dull assembly.
Boredom is boring chicken sandwiches for lunch - again!
Boredom is doing your homework before tea.
Boredom is a tiresome way of life.

Carys Fletcher Charles (10)
St Mary's Catholic Primary School, Bridgend

The Dump Haikus

It's easy to dump
Someone has put up a sign
Who will stop it now?

The land is dirty
Jam jars sunk into the ground
Sticks and odds and ends.

Muddy, cold, smelly
Rotten, old smelly carpet
The dump is dirty.

No chance of living
But please who will stop it now!
We do not like this.

Lizzie Suffin (9)
St Mary's Catholic Primary School, Bridgend

Red

Red is a bright, magnificent colour that keeps you warm.
Red is grand, it makes me feel warm inside.
Red is the hot flames of a burning fire.
Red is majestic, the colour of the royal carpet for important people.
Red is the colour of anger when people are in a rage.
Red is the colour of our bright hot sun in the summertime.
Red is the sign of love on Valentine's Day.
Red is the swirling cape for the mad bulls to charge at.
Red is the colour of blood, reminding me of Jesus on the cross.
Red is the colour of our wonderful lives.

Shannon Owens (9)
St Mary's Catholic Primary School, Bridgend

Magic Spell!

Put the ingredients in a pot
Place it on a fire and boil it hot
A wing feather of a griffin
Scorched, bloody red dragon bone
Blood of a giant troll
A vein from a fairy's wing
A stashing of orang-utan hair
One dangerous scorpion sting
A lower lip of a cave troll
Spitting and hissing, double trouble
In the deep pot, bubble, bubble
Two pulses from a tarantula's body
One gallon of slimy ogre's snot
A crispy skull of a spider
A cup of mortal vomit
Two black ant brains
Three clumps of cat hairballs
Twenty slimy, black leeches
Cauldron bubble's spitting sound
Creatures spinning round and round
A thread of male spiderweb
Two violet veins from a mouse's heart
Half a metre of dragon's dry earwax
A pinch of fur off a hairy beast
Two litres of Minotaur blood
One jar of racoon's green, greasy snot
Four freshly slaughtered magic imp snouts
Say this spell out loud and clear
We want this universe to hear.

Class 5
Trelales Primary School

Courage

The colour is white, simple and fresh.
Try to be courageous, you can do it!
It sounds like the tap on your back,
People saying, 'Well done.'
Smells go from the smoke of the fire
To the flowers people give.
You're feeling butterflies go through your stomach
And it tastes like the sweetest sweet
You've had in a long time.

Lauren David (10)
Trelales Primary School

Red

Red is like blood dripping
Red smells like strawberries being eaten
Red is a wild colour
Red sounds like fire sparkling
Red's the dead one
Red tastes like a glass of cherryade
And sweet strawberry jam.

James Lee (8)
Trelales Primary School

Sadness

Black is the colour of sadness
Like the black darkness of the night sky
The taste of black pepper in my mouth
Black is the colour of a black-hearted pirate
The smell is like the raisins on a hot cross bun
Like an angry shark's eye which is ready to kill
It tastes like dark chocolate cake when others have none
Like a tyre on a car which has killed many people.

Jason Tarr (11)
Trelales Primary School

Love

Love is red
Onto I fall a red rose bed
It's like a boat sailing across a calm, smooth sea
Carrying all my dreams and me
The boy I love I have to see
And need him to be with me
It was love at first sight
I think of him day and night
It tastes like the summer delight
Of fresh strawberries and cream that makes you take flight
It's like a warm summer's evening
Now the sadness from me is leaving
It smells like roses
And children's freshly picked posies
It sounds like the sea on a warm summer's day
As it laps up the sand and everyone rushes in dismay
It feels so soft, so tender
Like finest silk so smooth, so slender.

Siobhan Sullivan (10)
Trelales Primary School

Love

Love is the colour of the powerful red,
Like the amber traffic light turning red.
Rushing thoughts confuse my mind,
Like a new boy lost in school.
Smelling the scent of her long dark hair,
Like the fresh smell of fresh flowers.
Hearing sounds of her voice echoing in my mind,
Like a bird singing in the morning.
Feeling love for the first time.

Sam Knight (11)
Trelales Primary School

Recipe For Boy Cake

Ingredients
One boy, a barrel of bananas
Two buckets of burning bamboo
Three crying, crunching crocodiles
One pair of scary, slippery slippers
One enormous smelly egg
One really rough Roman
One root of flowers
One mouthful of maggots
And a bath

Method
Put the boy in the bath
Add the bamboo, maggots and the smelly egg
Cover the Roman in flour and place next to the boy
Place the slippers on the boy's feet
Sprinkle over the bananas
Cook for 12 minutes until the boy screams.

Rhiannon Williams (7)
Trelales Primary School

Love

The colour of love is ruby red
Like your birthstone
The taste of love is a heart chocolate steaming
Like a ladybird crawling through the grass
The smell of love is a sparkling rose
Like a fist ready to punch someone
The sound of love is a Jacuzzi bubbling outside
Like Fairy Liquid washing the cutlery
The feeling of love is in the heart
Like your face going really red.

Chloe Bigmore (10)
Trelales Primary School

Beware Of Boys - Boy Cake

Ingredients

One bag of bamboo
One tower of terrible tomatoes
One bath tub
One bouncing ball
One well full of water
One load of leeks.

Method

1. Catch your boy.
2. Place him in the pot.
3. Stir in the bag of bamboo.
4. Toss the terrible tomatoes.
5. Sprinkle over the leeks to taste.
6. Boil for 2 hours until ready.

Sophie Jerrett (8)
Trelales Primary School

Love

Love is the colour of red
It is warm and cosy
It smells like candyfloss
It feels like your favourite pillow
And looks like sharing an ice cream
It is like a dream
The nicest dream you have ever had
It is like going on a perfect date
With the one you love
Love is amazing.

Alex Evans (10)
Trelales Primary School

Christmas Poetry

Taste
The golden, flaming, hot turkey
Covered with scrumptious gravy
In the red-hot oven

Hear
The choir singing their carols
Outside in the
Ice-cold air

See
The beautiful Christmas tree
With baubles and tinsel
And lots of presents underneath

Touch
The soft snow
It's ice-cold
And pure white

Smell
Smell the mouth-watering Christmas lunch
With gravy and turkey
And vegetables all around.

Hannah Turner (9)
Trelales Primary School

Boredom

Boredom is the colour black,
Dull and plain like the thoughts going through my mind.
It has no taste, no scent, nothing to set off my taste buds.
It smells scentless,
Just like the smell of an ordinary stroll in the park.
It's the sound of a song with only one note,
Like the constant spin of a never-ending washing machine.
It's the feeling of being locked in a cage,
Like being stranded on a desert island.

Elis Narbeth (10)
Trelales Primary School

Recipe For Boy Cake

(To serve to a very greedy wolf)

Ingredients
Seven towers of terrible tomatoes
Two blobs of butter
Four funnels of fine flour
Six sacks of silent sausages
Five buckets of bumpy bananas
One bouncy boy

Method
1. First catch your boy
2. Next put him in a bucket
3. Mix the tomatoes, butter, flour and sausages together
4. Pour over the boy
5. Sprinkle over the bananas
6. Bake in a hot oven for half an hour.

Alys Williams (7)
Trelales Primary School

Anger

Anger, the colour of death
Anger, the colour of red
Anger, the taste of fury
Anger, the taste of blood
Anger, the smell of death
Anger, the smell of the best
Anger, the sound of death
Anger, the sound of an explosion
Anger, the feeling of blood
Anger, the feeling of death.

Thomas Acton (10)
Trelales Primary School

Red

Red sounds like burning hot fire crackling.
Red feels like wobbling jelly on a plate.
Red looks like a terrible danger, warning you.
Red tastes like red tomatoes, round and juicy.
Red smells like sweet strawberries on a plate.

Emily Kerr (7)
Trelales Primary School

Anger

Anger is the colour red
Like a blazing fire
It smells hot and smoky
Like a burnt slice of toast
Sounds vicious and beastly
Like a troll without his dinner
It tastes fiery and flaming
Like chillies in a sizzling curry
It feels burning and blazing
Like the sun scorching in the sky.

Megan Thomas (11)
Trelales Primary School

Lilac

Lilac looks like the sunset in the summer with the clouds
crossing the sun as it goes down.
Lilac sounds like people enjoying themselves at a party.
Lilac feels like big, round, smooth, juicy plums.
Lilac tastes like great big grapes.
Lilac smells like sweet grape juice.

Harry Bennett (8)
Trelales Primary School

The Policeman

I'm the policeman
Looking after you,
I'm the policeman.
'How do you do?'

I'm the policeman:
'Stop right there!
Put your weapon down,
Your hands in the air!'

'Get down from that tree
You could break your arm,
Hold on carefully,
Don't come to any harm.'

I direct traffic
And give speeding fines.
I come straight away
When you dial 999.

I check for fingerprints
And write notes in my book.
I investigate the scene
And try to catch the crook.

Then when the thief is caught
And the cell door is closed,
I write my report
And change my clothes.

And I go back home
And I pour a cup of tea,
And I'm not the policeman:
Oh no! I'm *me.*

Class 3
Trelales Primary School

Haiku Poems

Indoor
Indoors it is warm
I was very unsteady
And very relaxed

Outdoor
Outdoors is it dark
Outdoors it is icy cold
I do not like it.

Charlotte Winstone-Cooper (9)
Trelales Primary School

Blue

Blue is the colour of waves banging on the wet rocks.
Blue feels like the breeze swirling towards you.
Blue tastes like the strong sea that melts into the water.
Blue sounds like the bluebirds humming away.
Blue smells like icing on a cake.
Blue looks like bluebells growing in the grass.

Lucy Phillips (8)
Trelales Primary School

Gold

Gold feels like the hot, burning sun glimmering on top of me
Gold sounds like a golden bird singing its love song
Gold tastes like the inside of an eggshell
Gold smells like a golden, juicy apple, all fresh
Gold looks like the beautiful moon shining in the summer sky.

Jordan Lee (7)
Trelales Primary School

Haiku Poems

Indoor
Warmth creeps down my spine
Like fire burning down the wood
It is comforting

Outdoor
Outside it is cold
Shivers creep down my cold spine
Like tarantulas.

Cerys Parkhouse (9)
Trelales Primary School

Autumn

A utumn times are dewy and wet
U nder the ground hedgehogs are asleep, the perfect, prickly pet
T rees are golden, crisp and red
U p in the trees the squirrel makes his cosy, soundless bed
M y favourite season is here, *yippee!*
N ow autumn is here, let's collect some bright, crackly leaves.

Libby Grindell (8)
Trelales Primary School

Christmas

Crackers go bang when you pull them
Happiness lasts until Santa comes home
Rudolph is leading the way
Icing on the cake melting as the time goes by
Shining stars flash all night
Tiny angels floating in the air
Love and joy is shared between us
Smiles upon our faces on a very special day.

Shelby Osborne (9)
Trelales Primary School

Bridgend

Bridgend reminds me of fish and chips
I get all angry, petrol from cars smells.
I am hungry, I am grumpy.
Then a gust of wind comes and it starts to rain.
Everyone is running, I get knocked over.
My mum is pulling me around.
The rain gets heavier and heavier.
The shop tills are slamming, doors are crashing.
My favourite shop, my mum does not let me in here.
She said the queue is out the door.
My mum saw her favourite shop, the queue was out the door too.
But we went in there.
I felt angry.
Back to the car at last.
Soaking.

Charlotte Llewellyn (8)
Trelales Primary School

The Gloom

The white clouds turn to grey
Soon the thunder comes its way
Wind crushed into the dripping, wet rain
As the electric lightning hits my brain
Going up and going down, lightning strikes across the sky
I hear the thunder as it's going bang
Rain is pouring on the floor
Powerful nature goes even more
Getting quiet, slowing down
The floors are drying up all across the town.

Demi Rees (9)
Trelales Primary School

The Storm

Lightning - a giant electrical gun
Shooting deadly threads of silver
Across the starless, ebony sky.

Thunder - driving down to earth
Its roar is deafening
As it crashes like an uncontrollable car
A cunning, black cloud.

Wind - exploding everything in its path
Resurrecting objects
Moving with tremendous speed.

Rain - dropping like bombs
Flooding all the streets
Gurgling down the drains
Rain, soggy droplets.

Callum Edmunds (10)
Trelales Primary School

The Storm

Thin golden lightning
Wriggling through the dark black clouds
Looking for something to strike
Sheeting rain
Tapping on the window
Flooding rivers and houses
The silent but violent thunder cackling like an evil witch
Wind howling raging at windows
Roaring through keyholes.

Lloyd Wilson (9)
Trelales Primary School

Haiku Poems

Outdoor
There is a big puff
The green trees rustle about
I felt so relaxed

Indoor
Inside the darkness
We listen for sound, but we
Cannot hear a thing.

Ashley Lewis (9)
Trelales Primary School

Bridgend

Bridgend is a bustling, noisy town
In the shops I hear ching, ching, ching in the till
And I can smell fish and chips, I ask my mum for some
She drags me away
As we go back to the car the rain starts to pour
Everybody runs, I fall over and hurt my leg
My mum is still dragging me by the arm.

This is town to me.

Alice Bent (8)
Trelales Primary School

The Storm

The hovering, jet-black, puffed up clouds roll across the gloomy sky
The raging, roaring thunder boosts its devastating energy
Preparing to make its crashing attack
The rain spits and slams down on the concrete floor
Flooding the street, gurgling down the drains
The thin, sharp, screaming lightning
Rampages through the sky like a troop of fireworks
Blitzing the clouds as fast as a speeding bullet.

Joshua O'Gorman (10)
Trelales Primary School

The Storm

The inky-black clouds make a rumbling sound
As you look up to see the starless sky
You hear the dogs bark
As you wonder if a frightening storm is here

The rain starts pelting down
You should run for cover
As thunder starts to groan
Quickly run for home

You look out the window shivering like mad
See lightning running across the sky like fireworks
Count how far away it is
By hearing an enormous growl.

Then all goes quiet
Rain stops and you see a tree on the ground
You go outside and the clouds open up
Sun shines in the sky, the storm is finished.

Brogan Hubber (9)
Trelales Primary School

The Storm

The storm starts just as a trickle of rain and wind
Smashing against the windows of hopeless houses
There is no light in the sky, just black
It is as if the sun has put out its roaring, hot flame
The wind gets stronger, howling with glee
Suddenly the rain comes down like a battle between cowboys
Firing their pistols
Then a flaming snake zigzags down the sky, hungry for destruction
The drums of the gods start banging, it is like a war in the clouds
Suddenly the rain and the wind calm down
And the sun breaks through its violent cage
And the storm ends.

Sam Williams (9)
Trelales Primary School

The Storm

The reflective blue sky soon turns black
As lightning is on its way
You see the lightning like silver strikes shooting across the sky

You hear the screaming wind
Which sounds like someone's in danger
The leaves are rustling
And the trees are shaking
And everyone's staying away

Now the thunder has gone away
The light blue sky
And the blazing sun
Soon appears again.

Rhianydd Llewellyn (10)
Trelales Primary School

Bridgend

The coldness of the wind hitting my chest
So powerful, pulling me back
In town you are never alone,
Busy, bustling streets
People chatter, tills clatter, babies scream
The smell of fish and chips and curry sauce
Exhaust fumes and perfume
Grey sky goes clatter, clatter
The rain comes down.

Amelia Jones (8)
Trelales Primary School

Wales

On March 1st we celebrate St David's Day
The patron saint of Wales
The girls holding daffodils, the boys in their caps
Enjoy Welsh cakes and bara brith whilst waving their flag
Their costumes remind us of days gone by
When the people were poor
But still proud of who they were.

Now there are fields where once there were mines
The sheep and the trees have reclaimed what was once there
On the beautiful sandy beaches
The seagulls join in with children on holiday
Having fun in the sun and a run in the sea.

In Cardiff city, the capital of Wales
Lives the Millennium Stadium, the centre for sport
As the dragon looks out from the flag
The Welsh wear their leeks while singing the anthem
Supporting their team whatever the outcome.

Dylan Thomas, that famous writer, wrote in the Welsh language
Of the beautiful of all that is Welsh
The mountains of Snowdonia are beautiful all year round
Whether covered in sunshine or snow on the ground.

In his Welsh accent Tom Jones does sing
Along with Shirley Bassey, their songs make the valleys ring
Catherine Zeta Jones may live in America
But home is where the heart is
And her heart is in Wales.

Jessica Blake (8)
West Park Primary School

Wales

Every year it's March the first
I am so excited
I think that I could burst

We all wear our Welsh costumes
showing leeks and daffodils
The Welsh flag is seen flying
on castles far and wide
and we sing our national anthem
standing side by side

Wales was famous for coal mines
black and cold and damp
the only reminder I have now
is my great grandfather's miner's lamp

Rugby is the game of Wales
that we love to watch and play
Cardiff's Millennium Stadium is the place
and it's not too far away

A favourite day out for the people of Wales
is at the Museum of Welsh Life
It tells the story of days gone by
when life was hard and full of strife

Though some of us may travel
and some of us may stay
we are all close together
on St David's Day.

Matthew Williams (8)
West Park Primary School

My Poem About Wales

The green, hilly mountains,
With flocks of pure white fur,
Sandy, golden beaches,
Filled with noisy tourists every year.

The ruby-red dragon,
Stomping around in the fields all day,
Listening to our famous singers,
As they shout out hits and play.

Then comes lunchtime,
When I'm ready for some cawl,
My mum gives me some laver bread,
Which really makes my stomach growl.

The marvellous, wonderful stories,
With sad or happy endings,
Tales of magical or romantic glory,
With heroes unaware of dangers pending.

Gareth Edwards, Zeta Jones, Dylan and John Charles,
Tom Jones, Owen Money and all their famous pals,
They grew up in our land showing what is best,
We must have God on our side, heaven help the rest.

We are so lucky in this land, surrounded by such beauty,
All the children born here, their parents call them cuties,
And I believe if God above could turn the clocks of time back,
He would proudly pull on a white shirt and become a Swansea Jack!

Meg Dennis (8)
West Park Primary School

Wales

St David's Day is here
March 1st every year
Celebrate how you like,
Welsh cakes, mmm, they're really nice!
We wear our costumes to school,
And sing lots of songs,
We have great fun
All day long!

I like the Welsh flag, it's really neat,
And the daffodils and the green leeks.
They are a part of Wales,
Along with all the legends and tales.
There are some great people as well,
Like Dylan Thomas and Tom Jones,
They make us proud,
To be Welsh you know!

Cardiff is our capital,
Where the Millennium Stadium is,
You can watch a game of rugby,
A live band or two,
What you do, it's up to you,
But however you decide to celebrate this day,
I think there's one thing we need to say,
Thank you
'Our Patron Saint'!

Jade-Lee Davies (9)
West Park Primary School

Wales

W ales is my home,
A nd I am happy here.
L ush green grass to play on,
E very day of the year.
S unny days are best,
when we eat ice cream on the pier.

Callum Reid (8)
West Park Primary School

A Poem About Wales

This Wales is such a wonderful place
It's the land of the dragon
The daffodil and the Celtic race
The coal is still here, but the mines are gone.

The Welsh are famous for rugby and singing
The chapels have been pulled down
But the schools are still standing.

Our patron saint's day is March the first
Saint David's his name and he lived long ago
But throughout the land his name is found
In churches and pubs if you've got a thirst.

This year Wales are going to win the Six Nations
We've got Colin Charvis, Gareth Thomas and Shane Williams
We'll beat England, Scotland and France
It's a while since we've won but we've got patience.

Benjamin Vance-Daniel (8)
West Park Primary School

Wales

W andering through fields of golden daffodils
A nd wondering what Mum is making for tea,
L aver bread, cawl and bara brith
E specially for me.
S nuggling round the fire and feeling sleepy.

I magining how coal miners must have felt
S hivering, black-faced and ready for bed.

T om Jones, Stereophonics and Dylan Thomas
H eroes and idols, made for dreaming
E yes glowing and hearts pounding.

B est of all St David's Day,
E xciting and enjoyable;
S inging hymns and knowing
T ogether we will keep the flag flying.

Danielle Kitney (9)
West Park Primary School

Wales Is The Place Where I Belong

Wales is a land of sport and song
Wales is grey with coal mines gone
Trees and beaches, grass and sky
Wales is a place where wild birds fly.

Wales is cawl and bara brith
Wales is cockles and laver bread
Daffodils, leeks and rolling hills
Wales is a land of dragons and tales.

Wales is sheep on mountains high
Wales is streams and rushing falls
Rusting wheels on crumbling shafts
Homely warmth from cottage hearths.

Wales is Saint David, cathedrals and castles
Wales is Eisteddfords, bards and Irdds
Dylan Thomas, Gareth Edwards, Shirley and Tom
Wales is the place where I belong.

Kieran Richards
West Park Primary School

About Wales

We have many great things in Wales
We have the Millennium Stadium which is in Cardiff, the capital city
And our rugby team
There are many great players such as JPR Williams
We have great singers, actors and actresses too
Many people in Wales speak the Welsh language
We also celebrate St David's Day
We dress up in Welsh costumes to celebrate the day
There are coal mines all over Wales
Where most men and young boys used to work many years ago
All the mines are not working anymore
Wales has beautiful green fields where you will see the sheep grazing.

Bradley Young (9)
West Park Primary School

Sporting Colours

Green grass, red shirts and goalposts
Green, white, red dragon flying
Giggs shoots, misses, crowds sighing

Wind, rain, a different game
Stars of old, Gareth scores, real Welsh gold
Conversion taken, no mistaking, legends told

A rounded field, boundary seen
Vetch green, whites, red ball flying
Maynard hits, ball soars, seagulls crying

Small white ball, struck well
Green grass, bunker trapped, gold sand flying
'Woosies' there, ball is safe, always trying

Long run, track and spikes
Crowds roar, stand on seats, cheer
Lyn is there, bounding on, doesn't hear

Whispered silence, lights dim, table green
White, red, black, balls of many hue
Shot in pocket from Terry Griffith's skilful cue.

Kyle Richards
West Park Primary School

Wales

Wales has the most beautiful scenery,
Full of daffodils and lots of greenery,
Mountains high that reach the sky,
Sheep that play and birds that fly.

Wales has the most beautiful beaches,
Sand and surf as far as it reaches,
Children play and adults stare,
Taking in the great Welsh air!

Lewis Oakley
West Park Primary School

Wales

Wales has rows of daffodils dancing in the breeze,
Snow-capped Snowdon sparkles and slowly begins to freeze.
The legends we tell around crackling fires of the tusk of Ysgithyrwyn,
Warm bowls of cawl, laver bread and cockles are just the right thing.
Golden beaches with squealing seagulls flying high and low,
Roars from the crowd at Millennium Stadium gives us all a glow.
The story goes of blood and magic, the Black Witch tale is one
                                                    so tragic.

We have a singer called Mr Tom Jones,
He wiggles his hips and hits the right tones.
Dame Shirley Bassey sings the high notes,
Aneurin Bevan, who worked for the votes.

Dylan Thomas wrote 'Under Milkwood'
Whilst Richard Burton on stage and screen stood.
Actors, writers, singers and sights,
Wales gives all this in a way that delights.

Christina Saines (9)
West Park Primary School

Wales

In Wales we celebrate St David's Day
On the 1st of March, not May.
We wear a yellow daffodil all the way to school,
It's really cool.
The red dragon was on the flag,
He was blowing fire across my bag.
We have mountains, big and tall,
And rugby that we play with the rugby ball.
I love to eat the Welsh cakes that Mummy bakes,
And I can share with my mates.
I do enjoy St David's Day,
Because I can shout hooray.

Luke Hemfrey
West Park Primary School

Images Of Wales

We have many legends and tales
Saint David is the saint of Wales
Many castles tall
Some quite small
Lots of valleys and hills
On saint's day we wear leeks or daffodils
Coal mines were deep
Snowdon is steep
Millions of sheep
Wales is great at singing
We are also good at winning
Rugby is our best game
Football sometimes is a shame
Our national anthem is the best
We sing with more pride than the rest
Welsh language is hard
Soothing poems from a bard
Seagulls sitting on the sandy floor
While the sea is lapping at the sandy shore
Sunday walks in the park
Hurry home before it gets dark
Merry tweeting birds
Listen to their sweet words
Quietly walk along
Don't distract them from their song
Home to lamb chops for my tea
What does Wales mean to me?
Wales has lots of places to roam
Wales is my home.

Rebecca Lewis (8)
West Park Primary School

Wales

The Welsh dragon is the symbol of Wales,
Cardiff is the capital city of the country.
The famous Millennium Stadium is one of the landmarks
of the city where rugby and football is played.
The Welsh wear red jerseys to play their sport.
Some people speak Welsh with different accents from north to south
and sing the national anthem in Welsh.
On St David's Day, March 1st, the Welsh costume is worn by girls
and boys wear Welsh jerseys with a leek or daffodil
pinned to the costume.
Wales is a land of green hills and meadows with lots of trees,
Where sheep, cows and other animals graze.
We have lots of mountains and our highest one in Snowdon,
There are also many rivers, streams and some waterfalls.
In Wales there is lots of wind, rain and bad weather.
Many years ago Wales was famous for its coal mines
but now they are all closed down.
We are known for our Welsh foods, they are cawl, Welsh cakes,
bara brith and laver bread.
Wales is famous for its poets, actors, singers, authors
and sports people, such as Dylan Thomas, Ioan Gruffyndd,
Tom Jones, Shirley Bassey, Colin Jackson, Ryan Giggs
and Neil Jenkins.

Daniel Thomas (8)
West Park Primary School

The Welsh Hills

The mountain tops so beautiful and green
In the warm, glistening sun it sets such a scene
Where the sheep roam in the open fields
Behind stone walls you see them shield
With crops of corn and daffodils
I love to walk among these hills.

Rhianne Nelson (8)
West Park Primary School

Wales

Wales has daffodils, but when it is winter it gets colder and colder,
The mountains are strong, but when it is winter they seem
almost gone,
The snow is ice falling from the sky.
When the people say their prayers they have to say goodbye,
The Welsh songs are sung loud, the townspeople hear the sound,
The sandy beaches shine in the sun, the little children have their fun,
The weather is calm in summer but now in winter it seems
a lot tougher.

Sheep as soft as cotton disappear over the valley,
Birds sing their song, their chests are as red as the dragon,
The farmer walks through the field,
Leaving a trail in the gorgeous green grass,
Leeks grow tall and fat.
People are in costume,
Ladies in bonnets, men wearing leeks,
The Welsh rugby team will not quit, they play at the stadium
to keep them fit,
The rabbits hop in their burrows hiding from hunting foxes,
They are not scared,
They are brave, they are Welsh.

Rebecca Hunt (8)
West Park Primary School

Catref

I live in Wales with green mountains and dales,
And the daffodils sway in the breeze.

You can see lots of sheep munching on long grass so sweet,
Wagging their long, fluffy tails.

You can walk along beaches, sandy and blue,
See dolphins jump and seals too.

There are coal mines so black and mountain tops white,
Castles and ruins, what a wonderful sight.

Lydia Sheppard (8)
West Park Primary School

All About Wales Poem

Snowdonia mountain stands high and tall
Bright yellow daffodils standing there
The green leeks waving in the wind
People came from afar to see Snowdonia, the Welsh mountain
Some try to climb up to the top
Others just enjoy a walk

Cardiff city is a wonderful place
People go to see rugby in the Millennium Stadium
Waving their red, white and green flags of a dragon
Others came to see Tom Jones sing his Welsh songs

At lunch we have cawl and delicious Welsh cakes
Walking across the sandy beaches
On March the first we all see the Welsh ladies in their Welsh costumes
And some people speak Welsh too

At the end becomes a rainy day
All over Wales
The beaches are all soggy
The best coal mines - gone.

Hannah Williams (9)
West Park Primary School

Wales

The people of Swansea went down to the sea
To gather some cockles to eat for their tea
They also eat cawl using lamb from the hills
While adding lots of leek to flavour it still
Then after they'd finish with a large teisenlap
While telling old legends with children on their lap
The miners would beaver both day and night
In pits so dark as if always night
With their blackened faces and Davey lamps
They'd finish their shifts looking like tramps
Wales is my country, my life and my home
I'd never think of leaving, I never would roam.

Christie Owen (9)
West Park Primary School

Wales - The Nation

There's many good things that come from Wales,
Like football teams, pop groups and home brewed ales.
But most of all the biggest thing is,
Ian Rush because he is the biz.
Take Gary Speed and Ryan Giggs,
Wales' two best players that there is.
There's Barry, Swansea, Wrexham too,
But most of all we like the blues.
When it comes to music we ain't done bad,
You've got Stereophonics and they are mad.
Shirley Bassey, Tom Jones as well,
That's all the music I can tell.
We've film stars and poets and many other stars,
You can see these people in cracking sports cars.
We have fields of green and lots of trees,
And if you come to Wales you can see most of these.

Lewis Tonner
West Park Primary School

Wales

March the first, St David's Day
A very important date
Red dragons, yellow daffodils and green and white leeks
Little girls in Welsh costumes eating Welsh cakes
Little boys in Welsh jerseys playing rugby
Wanting to be the next Gareth Edwards and JPR Williams
Cardiff, the capital city, with its old castle
Also the Millennium Stadium, home to rugby and football
The old market selling laver bread, cockles and bara brith
Wonderful museums, shops and pubs, Cardiff has it all
Famous people, Wales has the lot
Great singers like Tom Jones and Shirley Bassey
Cool bands - Stereophonics, Manics and The Lost Prophets
Even Catherine Zeta Jones, the Hollywood actress
All of them proud to be Welsh.

Rebecca Carys Hurn (9)
West Park Primary School

Wales

The Millennium Stadium, it's big and tall,
In Wales the Welsh people love their rugby,
And like to watch them all.

The Welsh flag is the emblem of our country,
The Welsh dragon is on the flag.
Wales' fields are long and green,
And makes our country beautiful.

Wales makes its own special food, like bara brith and cawl,
This is special because other countries make different foods.

Welsh legends tell scary stories, but they are not always true,
Wales had dragons and trolls many years ago,
So the mythical stories tell us.

We have singers like Bryn Tervil and Tom Jones
Who are very famous already,
But there are many young children
Who are hoping one day to be famous just like them . . .

Wales!

Chris Strong
West Park Primary School

Wales

Wales is my home with mountains and streams,
You get carried away and lost in your dreams.
Lush green grass and fields all around,
Where horses, sheep and cows are found.
We also have lots of sand and sea,
Where we spend all our summer playing happily.
And there's nowhere on Earth I'd rather be.
On March the first we celebrate a day of fun,
For it is Saint David's Day, everyone is likely to come.
With girls wearing daffodils and the boys wearing leeks,
And the birds sing sweetly with their little beaks.

Emma Parker
West Park Primary School

Wales

Welcome to Wales
Don't need to look far
To tell you a tale
About some Welsh stars

There's Owen Money
Now he's really funny
At the comedy club

And next Colin Jackson
Now he's a fast one
At the starting gun

If football's your game
Ryan Giggs is the name
Playing midfield for Wales

How about the Manic Street Preachers
Now they'd be great teachers
To learn to sing

The Stereophonics
What a cool band
Another great act
To come from our land

There's many more greats
So let's celebrate
Put on that red shirt
For March the 1st.

Tom Beale (9)
West Park Primary School